RSPB

GUIDE TO
BIRDWATCHING

PETER HAYMAN & MICHAEL EVERETT

with additional material by R A Hume and N W Cusa

D1486100

CHANCELLOR
PRESS

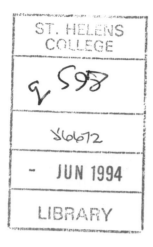
First published as *What's That Bird?* in 1977 by the
Royal Society for the Protection of Birds

This edition published in 1993 by Chancellor Press
an imprint of Reed Consumer Books Limited
Michelin House, 81 Fulham Road, London SW3 6RB
and Auckland, Melbourne, Singapore and Toronto

ISBN 1 85152 204 2

A CIP catalogue record for this book is available from
the British Library

Printed in China

Illustrations:
Page 6: David Hinchliffe
Page 7: Seabirds by Alan Harris
Page 9: David Hinchliffe
Page 11: Eleonora's falcons by John Busby

Contents

The Royal Society for the Protection of Birds

The Royal Society for the Protection of Birds is one of the world's leading conservation organisations. With a fast-growing membership, the RSPB's aim is to encourage conservation of wild birds by developing public interest in their beauty and place in nature.

The society's work includes scientific research, campaigning against developments that threaten the environment, enforcement of protection laws and the management of over 100 nature reserves. This work urgently needs your support.

For details of RSPB membership and information, write to RSPB, Dept N3091, The Lodge, Sandy, Bedfordshire SG19 2DL.

How to see Birds

There is no such thing as an 'instant birdwatcher' —
there are no short cuts to becoming reasonably
knowledgeable or to becoming fairly competent in bird
identification. Today's birdwatcher is mobile, well
equipped and well informed, vastly more so than his
counterpart of 25 years ago, but there is no fundamental
difference in the need to learn slowly and thoroughly,
and by experience.

I was sharply reminded of the 'basics' of bird
identification, and indeed of all the points Peter and I
were trying to put across in our embryo series, when, in
1978, I paid my first visit to the eastern United States.
Quite suddenly, I found myself amidst a whole host of
birds which looked and sounded unfamiliar. Indeed, in
the first 24 hours I encountered no fewer than 70 new
birds. I was right back in the shoes of the beginner,
with no quick and easy way of learning all these new
species, or of identifying most of them at first sight. So
it was back to first principles, slowly and carefully
learning shapes, methods of movement, colours and
calls — which is exactly how it should be.

So when and how should *you* begin? Birds are
everywhere, of course, but in the early days don't be
tempted to go too far afield. It is not necessary to rush
off to all the famous reserves and 'bird meccas' yet and
seeing a couple of hundred different species in your
first year won't make you a better birdwatcher. Begin at
home, in your garden or local park, or any other local
area to which you go regularly. Get to know all the birds
in your home area first of all — and get to know them
thoroughly. Begin by learning to recognise their
distinguishing marks — their basic colours, or patterns
of colours: wingbars, white outer-tail feathers, white
rumps and so on. Beware of males and females having
different plumages and remember too that juveniles
and immatures may look different again. Some birds
may even have different plumages at different times of
year. Noting *when* you see birds can also help in getting
to know them: some species are year-round residents,
others are present in summer or winter only and still
others merely pass through in the spring and autumn.

Shape and movement can be just as important as
colours and plumage patterns in bird identification.
Indeed, as you become more experienced you will find
that you will be able to identify some birds with
certainty simply by the way they fly, or run about on
the ground or sit in a tree, or by outline alone. Yet
another factor will be *where* your birds are: do they
stick to woodland, or only occur in open terrain; do
they occur on or beside water?

Build up your knowledge and experience by degrees,
but don't be misled into thinking once you've seen or
learned to recognise your local birds you should forget
about them. Continue to learn about them and get to
know them so well that you will be able to spot the
unusual when it occurs, or even the occasional rarity.
The working knowledge you have built up will be
invaluable as you begin the next phase, which is
moving further afield into your new areas and different
species in new situations. Spend time on these too and
try to 'learn' each new bird you see. Simply ticking off

birds on your list and moving on to find the next
species means missing opportunities to increase your
knowledge.

You will soon develop the knack of noticing plumage
features, colours and so on and with reference to
illustrations like those in this book you will 'learn' your
birds quite quickly and with increasing confidence.
But this is not the whole story: shape and movement
are vitally important too and it is no exaggeration to say
that the experienced birdwatcher can often make
accurate identifications on these features alone.

First of all, try and get some indication of size, not in
terms of inches and centimetres but in a relative sense.
Use a common bird you know well as your yardstick: is
the bird you are seeking to identify smaller than a
sparrow? Larger, but not so big as a blackbird? About
the size of a pigeon, a black-headed gull or a mallard?

And so on. Look next at its shape, and its general contours. It may be slender or plump. Or it may be long-necked or long-tailed; short-winged or long-winged; or with long or short legs — which can be an important feature in identifying some similar species (godwits, for example). The size, length and general shape of the bill can be one of the best recognition features of all.

Movements and postures present additional clues. Some birds shuffle along, like dunnocks. Sparrows hop, starlings have a characteristic waddle, sanderlings sprint along the beach like mad clockwork toys, plovers run, pause, and run again; there are countless other examples. Look too at how birds fly — again, there are many variations. Big birds of prey glide, kingfishers appear to fly in a continuous series of short spurts and woodpeckers have a characteristic bounding or deeply undulating flight. Fieldfares 'shoot' on closed wings between periods of flapping and sparrowhawks have an instantly recognisable way of flying with rapid wingbeats interspersed with glides.

Even the way a bird sits or perches can be an instant give-away. Short-eared owls normally sit horizontally, not bolt upright like other owls. Some birds stay in cover, or close to it, while others, like shrikes, corn buntings and many birds of prey, seem to select the most exposed and obvious perch they can find. Geese and gulls sit stern-high on the water, while divers and cormorants may adopt such a low posture that their backs seem almost awash. Coots and diving-ducks have rounded sterns, while the surface-feeding ducks are more 'cocked-up' at the rear. Note too how birds like mallard and teal can spring clear of the water to take flight, while grebes, coots and diving ducks have to patter along the surface with their feet to get airborne.

Older books made much of 'fieldcraft', which they possibly exaggerated in terms of its importance, but it is a valid part of birdwatching. It is really something you learn by experience, or by watching others, but a few general points can be made here. The essence of good fieldcraft is all about not disturbing your quarry and working to get good views of birds behaving naturally. It means moving fairly slowly and carefully, making sensible use of cover and trying to be as unobtrusive as possible. Avoid sudden appearances and watch from below the skyline (as the bird sees it) rather than on top — merge with your background as best you can and avoid sudden movements. Be prepared to stop frequently to watch and listen — half-an-hour spent sitting in one spot can often produce very good results. Birdwatching should be a leisurely and patient pursuit, with attention to detail, not a business of rushing all over the place! It should also be a quiet affair — there is nothing more annoying than birdwatchers who chatter constantly in loud voices, or who take no notice of where they put their feet (in woodland, for instance, try to go around twigs and branches, not over them!). There can be few things as satisfying as the long, patient and careful stalk which ends in prolonged views of a difficult bird.

Today's beginner has a difficult job in deciding what clothing and equipment to use: the variety on offer is simply bewildering. As in many aspects of birdwatching, much depends on your pocket and your

personal preference. Some birdwatchers seem to take a perverse pride in being as scruffy as possible, which is fine if it makes them feel happy and comfortable. Others dress in the latest gear and always seem to own the newest and most spectacular binoculars and telescopes — this is fine too. Most of us compromise with a position somewhere between these extremes.

What you wear doesn't matter very much, as long as you are warm when you need to be, waterproof to some extent and, above all, comfortable. Perhaps the only other important considerations are the general wear and tear on your clothes (and the likelihood that they will get dirty), which means old or tough outdoor apparel. Choose clothing in 'natural' rather than vivid and conspicuous colours, which does not make an inordinate amount of noise as you move about and with lots of pockets. Strong, warm, comfortable footwear is obviously of great importance: boots and shoes should also be reliably waterproof. It is worth choosing a pair of really warm gloves too.

I am not going to recommend any particular makes of binoculars. There is a huge range of generally suitable glasses on the market and what you choose is basically a matter of what you can afford. The small, lightweight roof-prism binoculars at the top end of the price range are excellent and optically superb — well worth the investment if you can afford them — but lower down the financial scale there are many more 'traditional' kinds which are very good indeed. Most birdwatchers opt for a magnification of between 8 and 10: there is no point in going higher. All binoculars are marked with figures like 10×50, which means the magnification is ten times and the diameter of the object (large) lens is 50 mm. The light-gathering potential of binoculars is important and as a simple test you can divide the object lens figure by the magnification figure for a candle 'value' in this respect. If the answer is around 5 (it is exactly 5 with a 10×50 pair), and certainly not lower than 4, the binoculars are suitable for birdwatching.

When buying your binoculars, consider their weight, whether you can 'handle' them and whether the eyepieces are comfortable — especially if you wear spectacles. Make sure they are reasonably robust too — this is more important than what they look like! Never buy by mail order, but go along to a reputable dealer and try out several pairs: don't buy the first you pick up. Make sure they focus accurately and that you have a crystal-clear image and beware of distortion and 'rainbow effects' at the edges of the field of view. Avoid zoom-lenses and choose something with simple strong working parts. The best thing of all to do is to seek the advice of a more knowledgeable birdwatcher before you make your purchase; better still, persuade him or her to come along to the shop with you. Binoculars are the single most important piece of equipment a birdwatcher owns and it is well worth going to a lot of trouble to get the right pair.

Many birdwatchers use modern prismatic telescopes, of which there are several good makes available. They are difficult to use until you gain some experience with them, but an indispensable item if you intend to go on and become a serious and active birdwatcher. Here it is particularly important to seek help and advice before deciding what to buy. Most people use a lightweight,

collapsible tripod, which again takes some getting used to but is strongly recommended.

No birdwatcher should be without a field notebook, which you should regard as being almost as vital as binoculars. Relying on your memory is dangerous — you will very quickly discover that writing it down is much better than trying to keep it all in your head! Record what you see, when and where, but do not regard your notebook as simply somewhere to list what you have seen. Bird-listing can be good fun, but there is rather more to birdwatching than simply making lists and keeping scores. Make notes on all the new things you see and hear, with details of habitats, movements and plumage features. Try and take full field descriptions of new birds you encounter, noting as much detail as you can. This is certainly an acquired art and one which becomes easier with practice and experience — but it *can* be acquired and you will find it immensely useful. One way to gain experience is to begin with some everyday birds: try writing a detailed description of a blue tit or a chaffinch — or, for a real and surprisingly interesting challenge, of male and female house sparrows! Many field guides will show you how to 'name the parts' on a bird: study the diagrams, learn the names of the different parts or groups of feathers and try to relate these to the birds you are watching. It will be hard at first, but you will be surprised at how quickly you can come to terms with supercilia, primary coverts and so on! Another very

useful way to describe birds is by producing simple field-sketches and annotating them to show plumage details and other interesting features. Don't worry if your drawings are not like Peter Hayman's! Very few of us have his talent and in any case, as he would be the first to tell you, yours are intended as quick reference sketches and not works of art.

Many bird books are called 'pocket' or 'field' guides, but it is best not to refer to them while you are actually looking for birds. A much better way is to make notes and drawings and look at the book afterwards — in this way you will teach yourself to notice and record the all important small details and you will also avoid the all too common pitfall of jumping to the wrong conclusions or trying to make your bird fit a picture in the book. All of this leads to misidentification. You will have noticed that we have made this volume too big for your pocket! A list of the bird books we recommend for your 'library' appears on page 12.

On the same page are recommended some records and tapes of bird songs and calls. These are a useful aid to identification, but nothing can quite replace a carefully acquired bank of personal experience: it is vitally important to find out about and learn bird calls and songs, which can often be crucial in bird identification. As with looking, so with listening: begin with your local species, learning their songs and the different calls thoroughly, at the same time noting when and why the different calls are given. Then expand your knowledge as you move further afield. One of the best ways of all to learn calls and songs is to go out with someone who really knows them — many experienced birdwatchers can identify birds by call with little difficulty and a day in the field with such a person can be worth more than hours of tapes and records, or deciphering the phonetic renderings in your bird books.

Thousands of other people enjoy birdwatching, as you will quickly discover. Get to know some of them by joining a local RSPB members' group, bird club or natural history society. If there are extra-mural classes in ornithology in your area, why not join in? You will learn a lot. Meeting others who share your interest is a worthwhile end in itself, but it will also enable you to go birdwatching with them — and to meet experienced observers. Learn all you can from these people, at every opportunity, because there is no better way of learning than from someone who knows what he is talking about. Don't be embarrassed because you are a beginner: ask for help and advice — you will be pleasantly surprised at how willing people will be to help you with bird identification.

Finally, never be dismayed if you cannot put a name to a bird. The honest birdwatcher, however expert, will admit that he will not be able to identify every bird he sees (or hears). He too will make mistakes, just as you are bound to do. That is all part of the fun of birdwatching.

Continental birdwatching

On pages 63-78, we turn our attention to some continental birds. A few of them also breed in Britain in very small numbers; many others occur as rare visitors. Rather than thinking of a strictly birdwatching holiday, perhaps with one of the many firms specialising in such things, we have treated this section as one dealing with some of the birds likely to be encountered on a typical family holiday. We have chosen an area 'somewhere in the western Mediterranean', including such habitats as maquis scrubland, vineyards, olive-groves, cultivated hillsides, conifer forests and wetlands.

Although the really exotic-looking birds such as bee-eaters, rollers and hoopoes present no identification problems, in several instances, where continental races replace our British birds, there are more subtle differences. It is always worth giving larks, wagtails and even sparrows a second look! The white wagtail replaces our pied wagtail in the Mediterranean and there are several different races of 'yellow' wagtails, while our familiar skylark is joined by crested and possibly also Thekla larks (a very confusing pair which are not quite so straightforward in the field as our captions might suggest!) The small and surprisingly sparrow-like short-toed lark is rather easier to identify.

As with all birdwatching, much of the art lies in knowing where to look. Scan roadside wires for rollers and shrikes and keep a sharp eye open for hoopoes, which despite their unique appearance, can be notoriously hard to spot on the ground. (The first you usually see of one is when it gets up and flies away on its big, butterfly wings.)

Almost any wet spot might hold little egrets, which are very conspicuous. Look out for the stockier cattle egret in drier situations and among grazing livestock. White storks are so distinctive as to call for no further comment. The same can be said for the flamingos, which occur in thousands in the Rhône Delta area in southern France, but may also be found in a few areas in southern Spain. Note how the purple heron differs from our familiar grey heron — it is smaller, darker and more angular in outline. Night herons are easily distinguishable but, because they are often most active towards dusk, easily overlooked. Watch out for the distinctive squacco heron and also the tiny little bittern, a bird most likely to be seen when flushed from cover.

Gulls are not particularly numerous in much of the western Mediterranean — but well worth a second look. The local herring gulls have yellow legs (ours have pinkish legs); slender-billed gulls are a possibility and southern Mallorca (and other parts of the Balearic Islands) might well produce the rare Audouin's gull. Both gull-billed terns and black-winged stilts are easily distinguished, as are two ducks occurring in this region – red-crested pochard and ferruginous duck. The various wetland warblers do form a difficult group and require careful study. The easiest to identify are the huge and raucous-voiced great reed warbler and the tiny fan-tailed warbler, with its monotonous song.

One Mediterranean speciality is the tiny scops owl. Its monotonous, bell-like, one-note song might be heard on early summer evenings; later in the year you might be lucky enough to see one hunting moths and large insects in a square or an area of large gardens.

There are several other birds of prey to watch for, such as lesser kestrels, which can be easily confused with our kestrel. However, while either species may be seen singly, the lesser kestrel is often gregarious and can be seen around tall church towers and other large buildings, where it nests in colonies. The sinister-looking black kite might be encountered almost anywhere, including town edges and at rubbish tips, but red kites generally prefer more wooded country. Egyptian vultures visit tips too, but are perhaps more likely to be seen where there are hills inland. Really high country means big vultures — griffons in mainland Spain and, if you are very lucky, the rare black vulture. The latter still maintains a tenuous foothold in northern and north-eastern Mallorca, where it is more easily seen.

Mallorca certainly has a lot to offer the birdwatcher. It is still a good place to see coastal-nesting ospreys which are quite rare in other parts of the western Mediterranean, and of course it is the place to see the star raptor of the region — Eleonora's falcon. Look for this dashing bird around high coastal cliffs, but watch for it too over fields and wet spots in the evenings.

These pages cannot cover every species you may encounter but they should give you a good introduction to the more common ones and we hope they whet your appetite for more birdwatching!

Right: Mallorca's speciality — Eleonora's falcon.

Books

Birds of Britain and Europe with North Africa and the Middle East by Hermann Heinzel, Richard Fitter and John Parslow. Published by Collins. Practical paperback guide, covering almost all the species to be found in Europe, the Middle East and North Africa. Excellent distribution maps.

Field Guide to the Birds of Britain and Europe by Roger Peterson, Guy Mountfort and P A D Hollom. Published by Collins. Although the oldest field-guide it is probably the best illustrated.

Hamlyn Guide to Birds of Britain and Europe by Bertel Bruun & Arthur Singer. Published by Hamlyn. Paperback with illustrations opposite the text.

The Shell Guide to the Birds of Britain and Ireland by Ferguson-Lees, Willis and Sharrock. Published by Michael Joseph. Excellent guide for the more advanced birdwatcher.

Popular Handbook of British Birds by P A D Hollom. Published by Witherby. Excellent source of background information about birds.

RSPB Guide to British Birds by David Saunders, illustrated by N W Cusa and Peter Hayman. Published by Hamlyn in association with the RSPB. Best field-guide for the novice because it is restricted to British species and thus avoids confusion.

Birds of Britain and Europe by Nicholas Hammond and Michael Everett. Published by Pan. Illustrated with photographs. Useful to confirm identification.

Watching Birds by James Fisher and Jim Flegg. Published by T & A D Poyser.

Birdwatchers' Code of Conduct

Today's birdwatchers are a powerful force for nature conservation. The number of those of us interested in birds rises continually and it is vital that we take seriously our responsibility to avoid any harm to birds.

We must also present a responsible image to non-birdwatchers who may be affected by our activities and particularly those on whose sympathy and support the future of birds may rest.

There are 10 points to bear in mind:
1. **The welfare of birds must come first.**
2. **Habitat must be protected.**
3. **Keep disturbance to birds and their habitat to a minimum.**
4. **When you find a rare bird think carefully about whom you should tell.**
5. **Do not harass rare migrants.**
6. **Abide by the Wildlife and Countryside Act, 1981 at all times.**
7. **Respect the rights of landowners.**
8. **Respect the rights of other people in the countryside.**
9. **Make your records available to the local bird recorder.**
10. **Behave abroad as you would when birdwatching at home.**

Welfare of birds must come first
Whether your particular interest is photography, ringing, sound recording, scientific study or just birdwatching, remember that the welfare of the bird must always come first.

Habitat protection
Its habitat is vital to a bird and therefore we must ensure that our activities do not cause damage.

Keep disturbance to a minimum
Birds' tolerance of disturbance varies between species and seasons. Therefore, it is safer to keep all disturbance to a minimum. No birds should be disturbed from the nest in case opportunities for predators to take eggs or young are increased. In very cold weather disturbance to birds may cause them to use vital energy at a time when food is difficult to find. Wildfowlers already impose bans during cold weather: birdwatchers should exercise similar discretion.

Rare breeding birds
If you discover a rare bird breeding and feel that protection is necessary, inform the appropriate RSPB Regional Office, or the Species Protection Department at The Lodge. Otherwise it is best in almost all circumstances to keep the record strictly secret in order to avoid disturbance by other birdwatchers and attacks by egg-collectors. Never visit known sites of rare breeding birds unless they are adequately protected. Even your presence may give away the site to others and cause so many other visitors that the birds may fail to breed successfully.

Disturbance at or near the nest of species listed on the First Schedule of the Wildlife and Countryside Act, 1981 is a criminal offence.

Copies of *Information About Birds and the Law* are obtainable from the RSPB, The Lodge, Sandy, Beds SG19 2DL .

Rare migrants
Rare migrants or vagrants must not be harassed. If you discover one, consider the circumstances carefully before telling anyone. Will an influx of birdwatchers disturb the bird or others in the area? Will the habitat be damaged? Will problems be caused with the landowner?

Wildlife and Countryside Act, 1981
Protection laws are the result of hard campaigning by previous generations of birdwatchers and other naturalists. As birdwatchers we must abide by them at all times and not allow them to fall into disrepute.

Respect the rights of landowners
The wishes of landowners and occupiers of land must be respected. Do not enter land without permission. Comply with permit schemes. If you are leading a group, do give advance notice of the visit, even if a formal permit scheme is not in operation. Always obey the Country Code.

Respect the rights of other people
Have proper consideration for other birdwatchers. Try not to disrupt their activities or scare the birds they are watching. There are many other people who also use the countryside. Do not interfere with their activities and, if it seems that what they are doing is causing unnecessary disturbance to birds, do try to take a balanced view. Flushing gulls when walking a dog on a beach may do little harm, while the same dog might be a serious disturbance at a tern colony. When pointing this out to a non-birdwatcher be courteous, but firm. The non-birdwatchers' goodwill towards birds must not be destroyed by the attitudes of birdwatchers.

Keeping records
Much of today's knowledge about birds is the result of meticulous record keeping by our predecessors. Make sure you help to add to tomorrow's knowledge by sending records to your county bird recorder.

Birdwatching abroad
Behave abroad as you would at home. This code should be firmly adhered to when abroad (whatever the local laws). Well behaved birdwatchers can be important ambassadors for bird protection.

This code has been drafted after consultation between the British Ornithologists' Union, British Trust for Ornithology, the Royal Society for the Protection of Birds, the Scottish Ornithologists' Club, the Wildfowl Trust and the Editors of British Birds.

Farmland in autumn and winter

Birds often form flocks in autumn. In flight these may be identified by the way in which the flocks are formed and fly. Look carefully at the flight patterns, the way in which birds move on the ground and at wing and tail patterns.

Woodpigeon in flight: note neck patch and white wing mark.

Below: **lapwings** in flight.

Rooks in flight: more swept wing and looser in manner than crow.

Woodpigeon

Stock dove

to show differences below.

Woodpigeon: large size, white neck patch.

Woodpigeon: large size, white neck and wing patches, pink breast.

Stock dove: note black wing edges, no white above and black wing marks.

Stock dove: "all" grey. Stocky but finer shape than wood pigeon and shorter tail.

Woodpigeon, stock and **collared doves** in flight to show typical flight positions. Note straight wing of **stock dove** with short, dumpy build. Long tail and swept wing of **collared dove.**

Pale wing panels (compare with **Woodpigeon**)

Collared dove: long tail, and grey and buff pattern unique in winter pigeons.

Swept-wing flight with flicky action unique.

Collared dove: note black collar.

Above (small) **jackdaw,** and rounded tail of **rook** shown in flight.

Jackdaw, rook and **carrion crow.** Crow squarer and more deliberate than **rook** in flight. **Jackdaw** quite jerky flight.

Rook: high forehead, bare face, trousered legs.

Carrion crow: all black, stout with clean legs.

Jackdaw: grey nape, small, perky action.

14

At night **barn owl** can look almost white in car headlights.

Pheasant: female smaller than male, buff coloured, long tail.

Rear view of male when flushed. Rapid wingbeats followed by long glides.

Barn owls: legs sometimes dangle in flight. All white below but individuals vary above. Some whiter, others much greyer than this bird. Slow, wavery flight.

Note black eyes in all white face mask.

Pheasant: male ring-necked variety. Red wattles. Long tail and bright plumage.

Below **grey partridge** in flight.

Grey partridge: male in flight. Note horseshoe patch or "blob" duller in female.

Moorhens are often found about field edges in winter. Flicking tail and flank stripe distinctive.

Red-legged partridge: red legs, striped flanks and face marks usually catch eye.

Grey partridge: male above has orange face, female duller. Compare difference in flank stripes with red-legged.

Red-legged partridge (above) rear and facing views.

From a car, **partridges** appear as round blobs in a field.

Lapwing: in flight and below. Black and white in flight: crest obvious on ground.

Above **red-legged partridge:** pale buff edges to feathers distinguish from partridge but difficult to see without practice.

Little owl: tiny, round-headed, undulating flight. Often on post.

Golden plover: above, typical flock shapes and lines.

Bullet head, yellowish, spotted plumage.

Golden plover: often alights (left) and shows wings before folding.

15

Thrushes and starlings in winter

All birds 1–7 drawn to scale

Blackbird: all black male (1) above. Brown female (2) below.

Starling (7) (above): blackish. Only bird to feed with open-bill probing.

Starling (right): characteristic sharp pointed shape; short, rounded tail.

Blackbird

Starling: pointed wings, short tail.

Blackbird: broad wings long tail.

Starling gliding.

Starlings (above) in typical, bustling feeding behaviour.

Redwing (3) (below): small, dark eye stripe, rather angry look and red flanks.

Song thrush: orange underwing noticeable in flight.

Fieldfare and **mistle thrush** (below) have somewhat similar flight.

More spotted breast than **redwing.**

Song thrush (4): yellower than redwing. No obvious head marks.

Redwing: small "red" wing, whiter underparts than song thrush.

Fieldfare: white underwing, buff breast, pale white belly.

Mistle thrush: large, broad wing. White underwing, "all spotted" body.

Mistle thrush (5): huge size, long tail and wings, boldly spotted breast. Looks greyer than song thrush.

Fieldfare (6): grey head and rump, reddish back and black tail unlike other thrushes. Call "chack".

Fieldfare (above) and **redwing** in flight showing pattern and typical flight posture.

Fieldfares: typical ragged flock.

Birds often seen in this position in the field.

Starlings: mass in flight over fields (below) and when off to roost. Thrushes usually in small flocks.

Fieldfare: grey head, rump, black tail.

Song thrush: overall yellow-brown.

Redwing: eyestripe, pale edges to wing feathers.

Mistle thrush: large size, note thin head. Pale rump and wing marks, white tips to tail.

Finches and similar birds in winter

All perched birds drawn to same scale

Corn bunting in flight: heavy wings, shorter tail and heavier head than skylark.

Flocks of mixed finches and buntings rise and fall over winter fields.

Above, **corn bunting:** large bulky bird, heavy bill and pale yellow-buff plumage.

Skylark: (above and left) small parties often fly low over fields. Note white outer tail feathers and white trailing edge to wing.

Skylark: compare size with finches. Fairly fine bill, buff with streaked plumage. Often crouches when feeding.

Skylark showing typical angled wings and triangular tail.

Dunnock (right): grey head, fine bill, brown streaked back, delicate feeding methods.

Tree sparrow (below): rufous crown, white black-spotted cheek and white collar. Sexes look alike.

Yellowhammer: instantly recognisable by bright rufous rump. White outer tail feathers.

House sparrow. Female above, male right. Country sparrows may be much brighter than city birds.

Greenfinch (left and above): stout, faint greenish colour. Yellow especially on sides of tail. Dull juvenile shown, adults brighter.

Chaffinch (female): wings as male but plumage buff and brown. Note slight "crest".

Chaffinch (male): blue-grey head, pinkish underparts and black and white wings.

Brambling: grey-black head, combination of orange and white in wing. Wing marks like chaffinch.

Brambling: only finch with chaffinch-like wing marks and white rump. Note no white to tip of tail.

Yellowhammer (juvenile): similar to female.

Above and right juvenile **linnet,** very small, slim, bouncing flight. Faint white edges to wing feathers.

Chaffinch (female): white wing and tail marks with greenish rump.

17

Finches and Buntings

Adults in good plumage are not difficult to identify — but look closely at the differences between linnet, twite and the redpolls, which can be confusing, and also at the female buntings: even experts find the cirl bunting and the yellowhammer difficult! Remember habits and movements too: these are very different in the superficially similar reed and Lapland buntings. Finally — don't forget the humble female house sparrow, which causes more wishful thinking than you'd believe. . . .

Brambling flying off: note wingbars, narrow white rump.

Brambling: characteristic greyish nape, orange "shoulders".

Winter male **brambling:** note head pattern, orange on breast and shoulders: compare wing-pattern with **chaffinch.**

Male **chaffinch:** blue-grey crown, brown back, white shoulder-patch, pinkish below.

Breeding male **brambling:** black, white and orange pattern.

Female **chaffinch:** dingier than female brambling, no orange; note wingbars.

Female **greenfinch:** duller than male, rather less yellow in wings and tail.

Male **chaffinch** overhead.

Brambling overhead: much paler than chaffinch, whiter under wings.

Juvenile **greenfinch:** streaky, but hints of green; yellow in wings and tail.

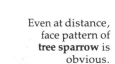

Even at distance, face pattern of **tree sparrow** is obvious.

Male **greenfinch:** bright green, pale bluish and yellow in wings.

Tree sparrow: smaller, neater than house sparrow (below) — chestnut crown, black spot on whitish cheek, white collar, small bib; sexes alike.

Male **greenfinch** note whitish bill short forked tail with much yellow

Female **greenfinches** on ground.

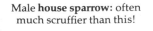

Male **house sparrow:** often much scruffier than this!

Female **house sparrow:** rather nondescript, but very variable: compare with female buntings. No white in tail.

Juvenile **house sparrow:** very like female, often more brightly marked.

Hawfinch from below: note black bib, width of bill.

Hawfinch on ground: dumpy, thick neck, grey nape, white wingbars.

Hawfinch: unmistakable if seen well; note white tip to tail.

From front, **hawfinch** has distinct face pattern — note eyes, black face, huge bill.

Juvenile **bullfinch:** lacks black cap and face.

Female **bullfinch:** sober colours, black cap and face, white wingbar and rump.

At all ages, **bullfinches** have black tails and white rumps.

Cirl bunting flying away: compare with yellowhammer (rt).

Yellowhammer: distinct chestnut rump in both sexes.

Male **bullfinch:** strikingly coloured even at a distance; bullfinches often feed at tips of branches.

Male **yellowhammer:** unmistakable; male yellow wagtail is unstreaked, slimmer, with fine bill.

Male **ortolan** (rare in UK): distinctive colours unlike any other British bunting.

Female **ortolan:** note pale eye-ring, pinkish bill.

Female **yellowhammer:** much greener than male, more streaked; chestnut rump.

Corn bunting: big, thickset, streaked brown.

Corn bunting sings from exposed perch— hedgetop, wires, fencepost etc.

Male **cirl bunting:** unmistakable combination of colours.

Female **cirl bunting:** very like yellowhammer, usually duller, no chestnut on rump.

Redpoll overhead: looks small, dark, with slim forked tail.

Redpoll: smaller and darker than linnet and twite; no white in tail.

Male **redpoll**: note red forehead, tiny black bib; pink or red on breast variable in amount.

Adult **redpoll** in worn, end of summer plumage — note pale underparts.

Male **redpoll**: dark, streaked upperparts.

Female **siskin**: much duller and streakier.

Northern or **"mealy" redpolls** are "frosted", showing much white, including on rump; rare **Arctic redpoll** (shown here) is seldom identified with certainty.

Male **siskin**: small, often acrobatic; streaky with black crown and face, yellow in wings and tail.

Female **crossbill** flying off: green rump, unmarked wings and tail.

Female **siskin**: note wing and tail pattern.

Male **serin**: distinctive small, streaky yellow and green bird. (Serin rare in UK.)

Female **serin**: small, streaky finch, lacking siskin's yellow in wings and tail but with yellowish rump.

Female **crossbill**: note green underparts, pale underwing.

Male **serin**: note yellow rump and compare with siskins.

Female **crossbill**: varying shades of green; feeds acrobatically in pines, larches etc.

Immature male **crossbills** are variable — combinations of yellowish-orange, red and green.

Scottish **crossbill** (Highlands only): heavy bill.

Parrot **crossbill** (rare UK): even heavier bill.

Juvenile **crossbill**: a rather pale, very streaky bird; big head, heavy bill, short tail.

Typical adult male **crossbill**: bright brick-red.

Juvenile **linnet:** note white in wings and tail.

Male **linnet:** grey head, variable amount of red on breast.

Female **linnet:** note rather plain head pattern, back only lightly streaked.

Juvenile **linnet:** much streakier than female: compare head patterns.

Juvenile **twite:** rather paler than juvenile linnet — compare head pattern, note leg colour.

Twite: looks darker than linnet, less white in wings; pinkish rump hard to see in the field.

Male **reed bunting:** black head and bib, white collar.

Male **reed bunting:** white collar obvious from rear.

Female **reed bunting:** note pattern of "moustaches". Fidgety action on ground.

Adult **twite:** streakier than female linnet, but paler below than juvenile linnet. Yellow bill, dingier in summer.

Adult **goldfinches:** unmistakable combination of colours; juveniles lack red and black on faces.

Juvenile **snow bunting:** some white in wings; note pale face pattern.

Lapland bunting: compare face pattern with reed bunting; note heavier build, short tail, long wings.

Snow buntings: obviously white below and on face, but very variable; all except juvenile show much white in wings. Shuffle close to ground.

Adult male **snow bunting** is whitest of all — unmistakable.

21

Woods, fields and gardens in summer

Buzzards: rear view (above) and three soaring in distance.

Kestrels: note pointed wings and long tail. Only small bird of prey which hovers habitually.

Buzzard soaring: note broad wings, short, well-rounded tail.

Sparrowhawk soaring: note long tail not fanned out and (below) diving from great height.

Buzzard gliding: tail and flight-feathers closed, note this is a darker individual.

Partridges: rapid flight with glides on down-curved wings. At distance (below) look round and dark.

Female **sparrowhawk:** note short rounded wings compared with kestrel. (Below left) going into dive.

Kestrel (above) and **sparrowhawk:** note relative shapes and proportions of wings and tails.

Common or **grey partridge:** note face and flank markings, and dark "horseshoe", much more obvious on males, barely visible on female.

Male **sparrowhawk:** mistle thrush-sized, orange below.

Collared dove: often tips forward and raises tail on landing.

Red-legged partridge: striking face-pattern and barring on flanks. Stripes over eye conspicuous even from rear.

Woodpigeon: largest pigeon. Note white crescents on wings, dark tip to ample tail.

Collared doves: compare with turtle dove (opposite page); much less contrast in plumage, different tail pattern and lacks striking white belly, wings more rounded, tail longer and flight less rapid and agile.

Woodpigeons: often rise with clatter of wings. Steady, fairly rapid flight, deep-chested appearance. In display fly up with noisy wingbeats, followed by short glide downwards.

Stock dove: blue-grey, smaller, darker, narrower winged than wood pigeon. Note dark border to wings, lacks white on rump seen on many feral pigeons.

Pheasant: some males lack white neck-ring. Female larger than partridge with longer neck, tail and legs.

Great (left) and **lesser spotted woodpecker** (centre) compared with **nuthatch** (right): all have rounded wings and markedly undulating flight.

Magpies: obvious long tail and white at wing-tips when flying.

Great spotted woodpecker: thrush-sized, strikingly pied; note "shoulder-patches".

Lesser spotted woodpecker: sparrow-sized barred above; often in very small trees among branches.

Magpie: only medium-sized, strikingly pied and long-tailed British bird.

Cuckoo: rather hawk-like. Does not hover, seldom glides. Wings flap below line of body, small head slightly above.

Jay below: note pinkish body, dark tail, wing-pattern, white rump and shape.

Jays: one bird flying out of wood is often followed by another; flight rather jerky.

Jackdaws: in flight all-dark; smaller than rooks or crows with faster wingbeats.

Male **green woodpecker** yellow below, green above red on head. Bill often pointing upwards.

Turtle doves: fast agile fliers, note white belly. From rear (above left) note chestnut wing-coverts and tail pattern.

Green woodpecker: rear view, note yellow rump.

Jackdaws: greyer than crows with dark crowns and "faces".

Female **green woodpecker:** habitually feeds on ground, very short legs, clumsy hops. Constantly turning head from side to side looking for danger.

Tawny owl: (left) characteristic upright stance and big, rounded head. Flight fairly slow and wholly silent. Note compactly built, big-headed, tail short and wings moderately long and rounded.

Male **chaffinch**: sings from tree perch, head back, repeated short song.

Chaffinch: male (above), female (right), note wing and tail pattern.

Male **greenfinch**: sings in "butterfly" display-flight overhead.

Song thrush: sings from high perch, continuous loud song, repetitive phrases.

Male **blackbird**: sings from trees, rooftops, etc; rich, languid song.

Male **greenfinch**: wheezes from tree, note (above) long wings and short tail in flight.

Starling: jumbled song with head turning and wings flapping.

Dunnocks: wing-flicking during display between pair.

Robin: usually sings from high perch, often in tree.

Starling: jaunty, waddling gait, probing with bill.

Starlings: glide in to land.

Song thrush: pauses between movements on ground.

Starling: also has upright waddle, compare blackbird (right).

Blackbirds: swing down in jerky flight, cock tail on landing (female shown).

Blackbird: hops or runs, males often follow-chase in long runs across ground.

Male **robin**: sings defiance at nearby rival.

Robin: pauses to listen while feeding on ground.

House sparrows: male (above) in low posture, female (below) in alert, upright hop.

Dunnock: "creeps" close to ground, flicking tail.

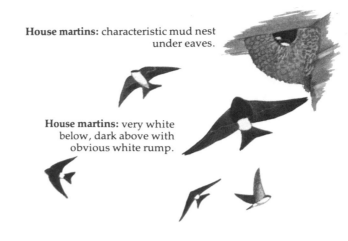

House martins: characteristic mud nest under eaves.

House martins: very white below, dark above with obvious white rump.

Swifts: aerial, fast-moving, all-dark and very long-winged; often in or over built-up areas.

Swallows: habitually fly low and fast, feeding over fields and water.

Swallow: from below, note throat pattern and tail streamers.

Skylark: "hangs" high overhead in continuous song and, (right) descends and finally dives to ground.

Mistle thrush: in flight, large, heavy and long-tailed, note whitish underwing.

Mistle thrush: larger than song thrush, less spotted below; sings from high tree.

Skylark: rear view, note wing shape, white rear edge to wings and white outer tail-feathers.

Skylark: (above) alert on post, crest raised, (below) low profile while feeding.

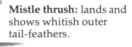

Mistle thrush: lands and shows whitish outer tail-feathers.

Mistle thrush: bold, often upright stance: often on playing-fields, in parks, etc.

Tree pipit's song flight: ascends and "parachutes" back to same or new perch.

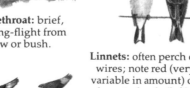

Male whitethroat: often secretive, but also appears and sings from exposed perch.

Male whitethroat: brief, dancing song-flight from hedgerow or bush.

Linnets: often perch on wires; note red (very variable in amount) on breast of male (left).

Linnets: in flight, note small size and white in wings and tail; open ground, roadsides, etc.

Tree pipits: rear and side views, very like meadow pipit but best distinguished by song, habitat and constant perching on trees, bushes, etc.

Yellowhammer: note long tail in flight.

Male yellowhammer: sings from exposed perch, often telegraph wires.

Wood warbler: usually sings high in trees, "vibrates" while doing so.

Male **blackcap:** often hard to spot singing in foliage, high or low.

Wood warbler: song-flights between branches, note long wings and yellow breast.

Willow warbler (left) and **chiffchaff** (above): feed and sing in trees, bushes, best distinguished by song.

Female **blackcap:** note brown cap.

Willow warbler: "hooeet" display near nest, keep away!

Blackcap: flies between trees, head pattern usually not seen.

Goldcrest: from below, tiny, short-tailed, crest often not visible.

Willow warbler or **chiffchaff:** often collects nest material on lawns, etc; note small size and distinctive shape.

Tree sparrow: black bib and cheek-spots, white cheeks.

Male **goldcrest:** orange crown only seen well in display, otherwise looks yellow.

Bullfinches: male (above), female (below); feeds on buds, often at very tips of branches.

Spotted flycatcher: uses all kinds of exposed perches, flies out after insects; note typical upright posture (right).

Spotted flycatcher: hovers to catch insect.

Male **yellowhammer:** rear view, note yellow head, russet rump, white outer tail-feathers.

Bullfinches: rear view, male (above), female (left), note white rump, black wings and tail.

Wren: very small, active, short cocked tail.

Tree sparrows: "dapper" appearance, brown crown and nape, black cheek-spot, note white collar.

Yellowhammers: feed on ground, low posture, often flick tails.

Great tits: male singing (left), less black on underside of female (right).

Nuthatch: near mud-adorned nest-hole.

Nuthatch: dumpy, big-headed, short-tailed; very agile on trees, can climb downwards.

Goldfinches: note wing-pattern (left), red face and breast patches from front (above).

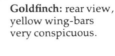

Treecreeper: flies from top of one tree to base of next, note wing-bar in flight.

Long-tailed tits: distinctive shape (below); parties fly in line across gaps in hedges, woods, etc.

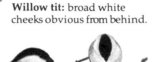

Goldfinch: rear view, yellow wing-bars very conspicuous.

Treecreeper: climbs jerkily, often spiralling as ascends trunk.

Willow tit: broad white cheeks obvious from behind.

Willow tit: note shape of head and cheek-patches, and pale wing-patch.

Coal tits: note head pattern, especially white "hole" on nape.

Marsh tits: with practice, distinguished from willow tit by shape of head and white on cheeks, but voice is usually best distinction between the two.

Blue tit: display flights from perch to perch, note wing shape.

Male **pied wagtails:** show aggression, note black back and long tail (below).

Blue tit: note face pattern and yellow underparts.

Blue tits: males display during battle on ground.

Male **pied wagtail:** aggressive posture, female has grey back; walks, runs, bobs head and wags tail.

Corn bunting: stout, rather nondescript, jangling song from bush, post, wires, etc.

Corn bunting: legs dangle as bird flies from song-post.

Corn bunting: rear view, looks heavy in flight.

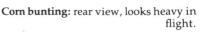

Warblers and similar birds

Many warblers are very alike at first glance, but a closer look often reveals subtle distinctions. Here we look at several species and compare them with other, rather similar-looking birds.

Melodious warbler (breeding): generally duller above, yellower below than icterine. Note shorter wing. (Rare in UK.)

Icterine warbler (breeding): note pale wing-panel, length of wing. Compare bill size with warblers below.

Icterine warbler (autumn juv): very yellow. Note pale wing-panel, long wings, orange edge to mandibles. (Rare in UK.)

Melodious warbler (adult): note dull appearance. Both melodious and icterine have heavy bills and pale patch in front of eye. Greyish legs.

Willow warbler (left), **chiffchaff** (right): compare head shape, eyestripe.

Chiffchaff (juv): yellower than adult, less so than willow: compare head shape and eyestripe.

Chiffchaff (spring): rather drab, little yellow. Note dark legs.

Willow warbler (juv): very yellow below, green above.

Willow warbler (adult): compare with spring chiffchaff. Note pale legs. Best told apart by song.

Chiffchaff (juv): note yellowish wash below.

Willow warbler/ chiffchaff in flight: look almost identical.

Willow warbler from below: compare with wood warbler (right).

Wood warbler: larger than willow or chiffchaff, very green-and-yellow, with white belly. Note long wings.

Wood warbler above: note yellow breast, white belly (compare with **willow**).

Reed warbler: brown above, whitish throat, long bill, non-stop varied song.

Fan-tailed warbler: tiny, short-tailed, "zip-zip-zip-zip . . ." in song flight overhead. (Rare in UK.)

Savi's warbler: very like large reed warbler. Note length and shape of tail. (Rare in UK.)

Typical **reed warbler:** often difficult to separate from marsh.

Marsh warbler: typical pale underparts. More musical song than reed, with even more mimicry. Usually the two only separable after much experience of both.

Savi's warbler: best told by voice — reeling, continuous song. (Rare in UK.)

Typical **marsh warbler:** often drabber brown, slightly longer wing, paler below. (Rare in UK.)

Fan-tailed warbler: tiny, streaked tawny and dark: note very distinctive tail.

Grasshopper warbler: more often heard than seen, but may sing in full view: long reeling song, like endless unwinding of angler's reel.

Flying into cover, **Cetti's** is very dark with ample, rounded tail.

Typical **grasshopper warbler:** note streaked crown and back, distinctive tail-shape.

Cetti's warbler: very skulking; short, explosive, loud song. Earth-brown above, distinct short pale eyestripe. (Rare in UK.)

Aquatic warbler: note contrast of tawny with dark streaks, light centre to crown, pointed tips to tail feathers. (Rare in UK.)

Grasshopper warbler: very variable — some are very buffish below.

Beware juvenile **sedge warbler** (left) — pale stripe in centre of crown might suggest **aquatic** (right) — which is much broader, more conspicuous.

Sedge warbler: streaked above, creamy eyestripe, harsher, less rhythmic song than reed.

Sedge warbler (juv): more tawny on rump than adult, head more distinctly streaked.

Aquatic warbler (below): much more contrasting pattern of streaks — rather yellower. Note rump actually has small streaks.

Sedge warbler (left): flying away — chestnut/tawny rump very conspicuous.

29

Spotted flycatcher (adult): upright stance, streaked crown and breast. No wingbar.

Spotted flycatcher (juv): more noticeably streaked and spotted than adult.

Pied flycatcher (male): unmistakable. Resembles female in autumn.

Pied flycatcher (female): note white wingbar and underparts.

Lesser whitethroat: note grey rump.

Lesser whitethroat (female): lacks pinkish wash below often seen on males.

Whitethroat (female): duller brown than male, lacks grey on head.

Lesser whitethroat (male): darker, neater than whitethroat, much greyer, often with dark ear-coverts.

Lesser whitethroat (autumn juv): browner than adult, but still darker than whitethroat.

Whitethroat (male): pale grey head, chestnut on back/wings, tawny rump.

Garden warbler: note pale buffish underparts, short bill.

Whitethroat: often sings in brief song-flight from hedge, wires etc.

Garden warbler: drab, featureless, round head, short bill, greyish legs. Larger than willow warbler or chiffchaff.

Blackcap (female): dull chestnut cap.

Blackcap (male): rather darker than female, black cap.

Dartford warbler (male): unmistakable if seen well. Note very long tail.

Flitting through cover, **Dartfords** look small, long-tailed, wholly dark.

Goldcrest from below: tiny, short-tailed, constantly moving.

Goldcrest from rear: note head and wing pattern (compare firecrest below).

Dartford warbler (female): much drabber than male. Note red eye.

Goldcrest (juv): lacks adult's head markings. Much tinier than warblers.

Goldcrest in flight: very small, short-tailed.

Wren: dumpy, short-tailed, mainly brown.

Goldcrest: note big eye. Crown often not easily visible.

Firecrest: greener than goldcrest, whiter below, bronze shoulder-patch.

Firecrest: very different head-pattern to goldcrest.

Dunnock: grey head, streaky back. Often shuffling along on ground.

Tree pipit has distinctive song: song-flight often from tree or bush.

Tree pipit: streaky, often yellower below than meadow pipit, pinker legs.

Meadow pipit: variable — often brownish, but see right. Note — almost same size as tree-pipit.

Meadow pipit — distinctive song, simpler than tree's. Song flight normally from ground.

Beware! **meadow pipits** also perch on bushes and small trees . . .

Meadow pipit — sometimes quite "greenish". Note not always slim posture.

Mountain and moorland in spring and summer

These species breed in uplands. Birds of prey are almost always first spotted in flight, when the important features to look for are shape, proportion of wings, body and tail and the way in which they fly. Eagles and buzzards, kestrels and merlins, ravens and crows are species likely to be confused.

Immature **golden eagle** and **buzzard** soaring: note size difference.

Immature **golden eagle**: all dark, varying amount of white in wings and at base of tail.

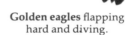

Eagle

Eagle　　　　　　　　　**Buzzard**

Golden eagle and **buzzard** soaring, and typical "going-away" view of eagle.

Golden eagle　　**Buzzard**

Raven

Adult **golden eagle**: all dark, note prominent head, ample tail and bulging rear edge on wing.
Buzzard: more compact, varying pattern on belly and underwing.
Raven: black, narrow-winged, distinctive tail-shape, buzzard-sized.

Golden eagles flapping hard and diving.

Immature **golden eagle** gliding: wings slightly back, tail half-open.

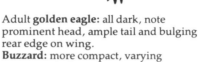

Red kite gliding: tail twists and flexes.

Near-adult **golden eagle** gliding fast: note wing shape.

Adult **golden eagle** hunting.

Carrion crow (left) and distinctive **hooded crow** (right): compare shape with raven.

Red kite: note colour, conspicuous pale wing-panels: longer-winged than buzzard, distinctive tail.

Golden eagles overhead, fast sailing or gliding: all dark, note prominence of head and length of tail.

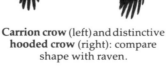

Ravens on ground: large, heavy, massive bill.

Ravens on wing: powerful, active fliers, acrobatic; diagnostic call "pruuk".

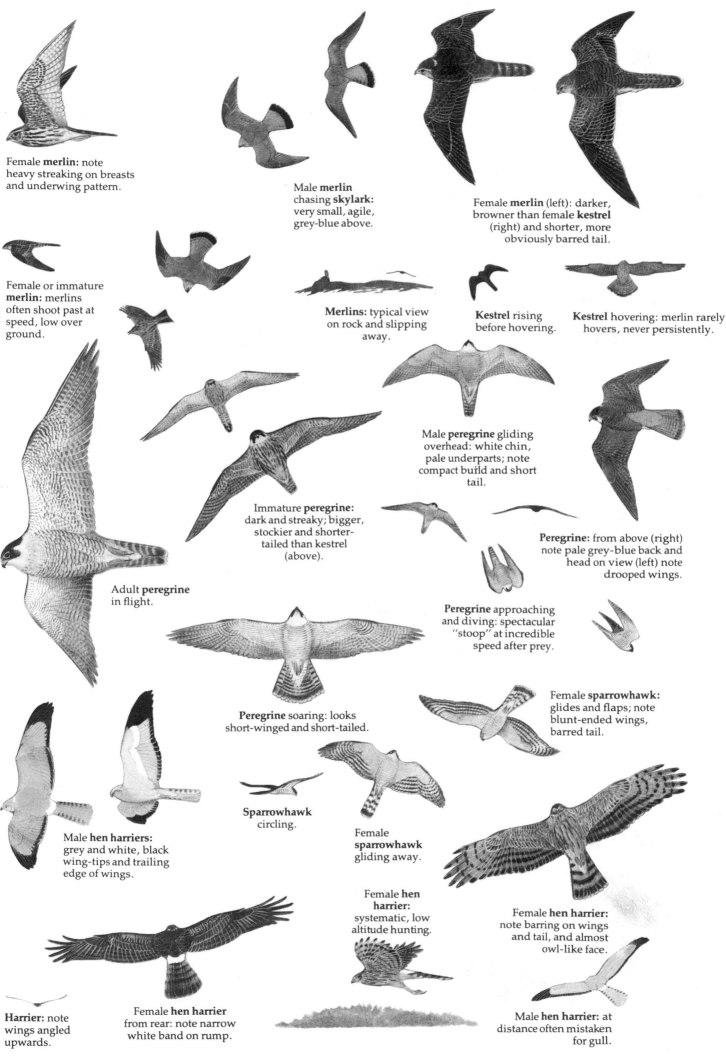

Female **merlin:** note heavy streaking on breasts and underwing pattern.

Male **merlin** chasing **skylark:** very small, agile, grey-blue above.

Female **merlin** (left): darker, browner than female **kestrel** (right) and shorter, more obviously barred tail.

Female or immature **merlin:** merlins often shoot past at speed, low over ground.

Merlins: typical view on rock and slipping away.

Kestrel rising before hovering.

Kestrel hovering: merlin rarely hovers, never persistently.

Male **peregrine** gliding overhead: white chin, pale underparts; note compact build and short tail.

Immature **peregrine:** dark and streaky; bigger, stockier and shorter-tailed than kestrel (above).

Peregrine: from above (right) note pale grey-blue back and head on view (left) note drooped wings.

Adult **peregrine** in flight.

Peregrine approaching and diving: spectacular "stoop" at incredible speed after prey.

Peregrine soaring: looks short-winged and short-tailed.

Female **sparrowhawk:** glides and flaps; note blunt-ended wings, barred tail.

Sparrowhawk circling.

Female **sparrowhawk** gliding away.

Male **hen harriers:** grey and white, black wing-tips and trailing edge of wings.

Female **hen harrier:** systematic, low altitude hunting.

Female **hen harrier:** note barring on wings and tail, and almost owl-like face.

Harrier: note wings angled upwards.

Female **hen harrier** from rear: note narrow white band on rump.

Male **hen harrier:** at distance often mistaken for gull.

33

Red grouse: plum pudding colour, found on heather moorland.

Red grouse approaching: note bowed wings.

Red grouse: often seen "gritting" at quiet roadsides.

Cock **red grouse.**

Ptarmigan: replace grouse on high mountains; tame, well camouflaged grey-and-white.

Ptarmigan: all white in winter, but have distinctive white wings at all seasons.

Red grouse: flushed and rocketing away, often calling.

Male and female **black grouse** overhead: both show white underwings.

Black grouse: both sexes perch readily in small trees.

Male **black grouse** (blackcock) rising: note white underwing, long tail.

Male **black grouse** from behind: white wing-bars, unique tail shape.

Female **black grouse** (greyhen): larger, greyer than red grouse, forked tail.

Female **black grouse** (greyhen): larger, greyer, larger-tailed than **red grouse.**

Curlew: distinctive bill, large size, very vocal.

Curlew from rear: note white rump, pale tail.

Curlew: typical view behind ridge.

Curlew: plumage camouflages bird on grass and moorland.

Golden plover going away: dark, slight wing-bar, very rapid flight.

Greenshank: note white rump in "v" up back, long bill, legs trail beyond tail.

Hooded crows: mainly found in west and north-west Scotland and Ireland; hybridises with carrion crow in central and eastern Highlands.

Short-eared owls: day-hunting, long-winged owls of open country. Note pale underwing, dark patch at bend of wing: frequently hover.

Golden plover: black on belly, pale underwing.

Golden plover: vary from well-marked northern form (left) to black-bellied southern form (right), but many intermediates.

Golden plover: gold-spangled upperparts, slight wing-bar.

Dotterel: note blackish crown and white eye-stripe.

Dotterel: note white breast-band, chestnut lower breast and dark belly.

Lapwing: often common on marginal uplands.

Red-throated diver (left): small lochs and pools; **black-throated** usually larger waters.

Dotterel: white eye-stripe and chin, very dark underparts.

Grey wagtail: note grey back, yellow on rump; found on hill streams.

Meadow pipit: note white outer tail-feathers.

Skylark singing.

Skylark from rear: white rear edge to wing, white outer tail-feathers.

Meadow pipit: streaky plumage, distinctive "tseep-tseep" calls.

Ring ouzels: note grey in wing-feathers, brownish female has pale crescent on breast; rocky hillsides.

Dunlin landing; distinct black belly in summer.

Wheatear: only small birds in these habitats with flashing white rump.

Twite: like dark female **linnet** but streakier, buff throat, yellowish bill.

Female **stonechat** (above) and female **whinchat** (below): note latter's wing and tail markings.

Dunlin in breeding plumage: chestnut above, note white wing-bars.

Common sandpipers: wings stiffly bowed in flight, conspicuous white wing-bars; streams and lake-sides.

Twite: male (right) compared with female (left) male's pinkish rump hard to see in field; distinctive nasal "twite" calls.

Female linnet: shows much more white in flight than twite.

Dipper found on or along rocky streams.

Birds of prey

The most many of us ever see of a bird of prey is a dark, rapidly-moving shape in the sky. Because they are usually only seen in flight, raptors are a difficult group for many birdwatchers, with some, such as the harriers, presenting particular problems. Often plumage details may not be visible, so look for shape and the way the bird flies.

Immature: dark, streaky; note white showing in tail-feathers.

Adult soaring: very broad wings, often very pale breast and head, short white tail.

White-tailed eagle

Compare immature (above) with adult **golden eagle** (below). White-tailed usually larger and bulkier,

with very prominent head and huge bill — but compare shape of wings and length and shape of tail.

Two head-on views of **white-tailed eagle**; usually soars on almost flat wings.

Carrion crow for comparison.

Heavy, flapping flight on take-off or when travelling short distances. Note very prominent head and bill.

At rest, often on ground or shore, white-tailed is big, rather untidy, sluggish-looking eagle.

Golden eagle

Immature darker than adult, big white flashes, white base to tail.

Near adult plumage showing white in tail and only traces of white in wings.

Adult: no white, straw-coloured crown and nape, paler wing-coverts.

Adult approaching: note pale head and wing-coverts.

Adult above observer: looks very dark (all black at distance or in poor light).

Usually soars with wings held slightly upwards.

Adult gliding on angled wings. Note trace of white in wings, pale crown and nape sometimes very conspicuous.

Female **sparrowhawk:** gliding down, circling and turning away. Compare shape with goshawk (left).

Immature **goshawk** overhead: much bigger and bulkier than sparrowhawk — size of buzzard.

Female **sparrowhawk:** blunt-ended wings, long tail.

Goshawk side view: flaps and glides. Note apparent dark cap, white undertail coverts.

Adult **goshawks** going away: note bulky shape, and white undertail often very obvious.

Goshawk: typical rear view of bird gliding away.

Peregrines overhead: robust build, relatively short wings, short tail.

Peregrine approaching: looks "anchor-shaped"; note dark face.

Adult **peregrine**: blue-grey above, black head: note distinctive shape.

Peregrine beginning "stoop" after prey.

Peregrine gliding fast on angled wings: note short tail.

Immature **peregrine**: note shape; largely dark brown.

Red-footed falcon: very small, hovers frequently.

Hobby approaching: white throat very obvious. Easy, elastic wingbeats.

Male **kestrel**: grey head and tail, chestnut back and wings.

Hobby may look dark or pale grey. Note head pattern, long wings, shorter tail than kestrel.

Red-footed falcon immature males (1 and 3). Variable. Streaked buffish below. Note pale collar, head pattern. Male (2).

Hobby: more rakish than kestrel, almost swift-like at times.

Immature **hobby** soaring: compare shape with kestrel below.

Hobby side view: note short tail, long wings, face pattern.

Hobby from below: conspicuous face pattern, streaked breast. Russet flanks not often conspicuous. Fast, very agile flier; rarely hovers.

Kestrel: compare with hobbies above.

Female **kestrel**: brown, mottled darker, with long, barred tail with pale tip.

Male **merlin**: tiny, blue-grey above, dark tail band.

Soaring **kestrel**: pale wing-linings, ample tail with dark band near tip.

Female **merlin**: browner than kestrel, tail barred creamy and brown.

Female **merlin** in typical low, dashing hunting flight.

37

Marsh harrier

Female or immature: all dark, varying amounts pale feathering on head.

In distance: all dark, varying amounts pale feathering on head.

Male: note underwing pattern.

Dark female/immature, showing creamy face and forewing.

Male: strikingly contrasted wing pattern, grey tail.

Soaring: compare with buzzards

Hunting: female often with obvious pale head and leading wing-edge. Note hanging feet.

Hen harrier

Female/immature birds — "ringtails". Hard to distinguish from Montagu's, but heavier build and flight; compare face pattern.

Male: very pale grey, black wingtip, white rump.

Ringtail: long wings, long tail, white rump.

Montagu's harrier

Usually spring-autumn only, now very rare in UK.

Male: light, buoyant flight, dark line across midwing.

Distant immature (left) and very rare melanistic female — like slim, lightweight immature marsh harrier.

Immature: diagnostic reddish underparts and underwing.

Male in transitional plumage: compare pattern with much bigger, bulkier marsh harrier (top left).

"Ringtail": difficult to tell from similar hen (above) — but normally much more marked face pattern.

Female: note pale ear-coverts with dark crescent behind.

Male has barred underwing, russet streaks on flanks.

Male: with good view, easily distinguished: compare with male hen harrier above.

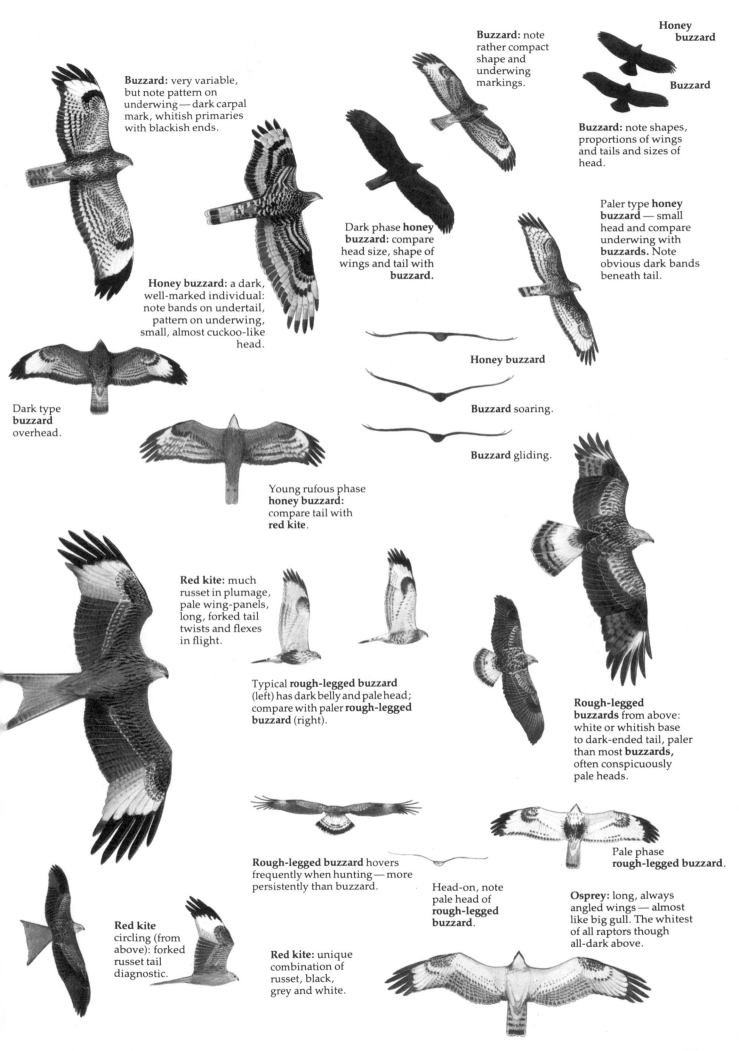

Buzzard: very variable, but note pattern on underwing — dark carpal mark, whitish primaries with blackish ends.

Honey buzzard: a dark, well-marked individual: note bands on undertail, pattern on underwing, small, almost cuckoo-like head.

Dark type **buzzard** overhead.

Buzzard: note rather compact shape and underwing markings.

Honey buzzard

Buzzard

Buzzard: note shapes, proportions of wings and tails and sizes of head.

Dark phase **honey buzzard:** compare head size, shape of wings and tail with **buzzard.**

Paler type **honey buzzard** — small head and compare underwing with **buzzards.** Note obvious dark bands beneath tail.

Honey buzzard

Buzzard soaring.

Buzzard gliding.

Young rufous phase **honey buzzard:** compare tail with **red kite.**

Red kite: much russet in plumage, pale wing-panels, long, forked tail twists and flexes in flight.

Typical **rough-legged buzzard** (left) has dark belly and pale head; compare with paler **rough-legged buzzard** (right).

Rough-legged buzzards from above: white or whitish base to dark-ended tail, paler than most **buzzards,** often conspicuously pale heads.

Red kite circling (from above): forked russet tail diagnostic.

Red kite: unique combination of russet, black, grey and white.

Rough-legged buzzard hovers frequently when hunting — more persistently than buzzard.

Head-on, note pale head of **rough-legged buzzard**.

Pale phase **rough-legged buzzard.**

Osprey: long, always angled wings — almost like big gull. The whitest of all raptors though all-dark above.

Coasts and cliffs in spring and summer

Waders in breeding plumage are boldly marked and quite easy to distinguish once their patterns have been learned. Terns require practice and patience. Although relatively easy at their breeding colonies, auks (puffin, razorbill and guillemots) are often difficult to identify when they are flying offshore.

Oystercatchers: large, pied, noisy birds.

Ringed plover: "butterfly" display flight.

Avocet: mostly white; unmistakable.

Ringed plover: sandy-brown above, white wing-bar.

Dunlin: streaked chestnut back, white wing-bars, longish bill.

Redshank: only medium-sized wader with white rump and hindwing; noisy.

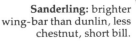

Sanderling: brighter wing-bar than dunlin, less chestnut, short bill.

Redshank: speckled brown, pale belly, obvious bright red legs.

Knot: medium-sized, mottled chestnut on back, faint white wing-bar.

Turnstone: unique black, white and chestnut pattern on wings and back.

Ringed plover: note head pattern and black breast-band; yellow legs.

Summer turnstone: unmistakable tortoise-shell pattern; note transitional plumage of sub-adult (right).

Knot: stocky, short-legged, pinkish to russet underparts.

Shelduck: unmistakable; looks pied, near goose-size.

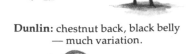

Dunlin: chestnut back, black belly — much variation.

Sanderling: white belly, short, straight black bill.

Rock pipit: dark, streaky olive-brown, dull greyish outer tail feathers (white in meadow pipit).

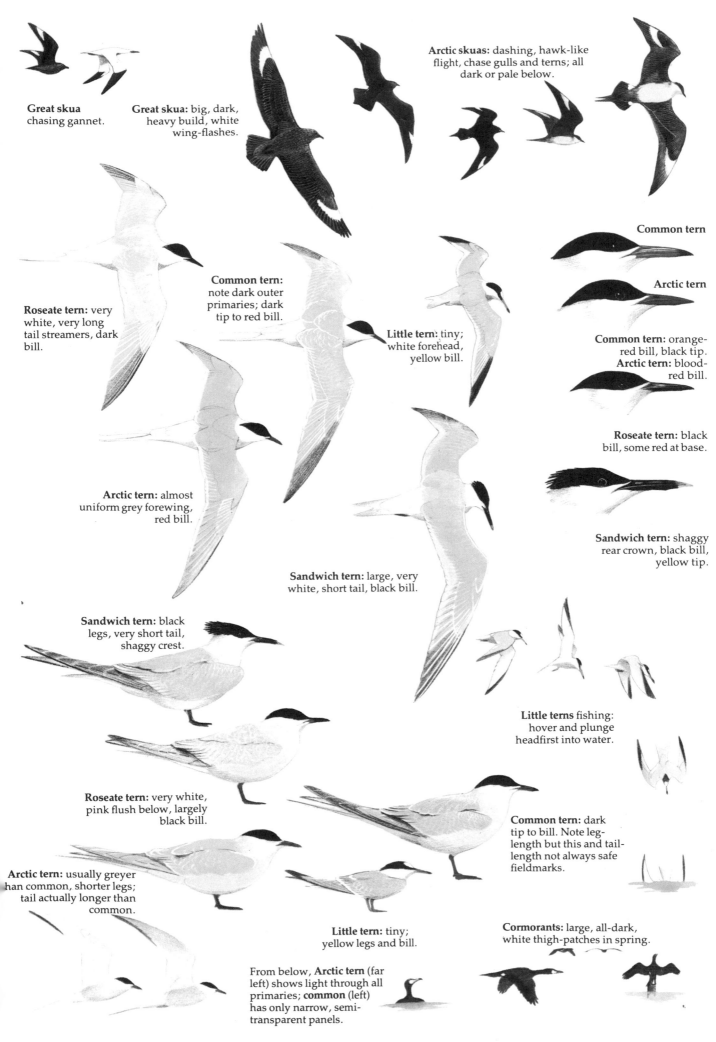

Great skua
chasing gannet.

Great skua: big, dark,
heavy build, white
wing-flashes.

Arctic skuas: dashing, hawk-like
flight, chase gulls and terns; all
dark or pale below.

Roseate tern: very
white, very long
tail streamers, dark
bill.

Common tern:
note dark outer
primaries; dark
tip to red bill.

Little tern: tiny;
white forehead,
yellow bill.

Common tern

Arctic tern

Common tern: oranged-
red bill, black tip.
Arctic tern: blood-
red bill.

Arctic tern: almost
uniform grey forewing,
red bill.

Roseate tern: black
bill, some red at base.

Sandwich tern: large, very
white, short tail, black bill.

Sandwich tern: shaggy
rear crown, black bill,
yellow tip.

Sandwich tern: black
legs, very short tail,
shaggy crest.

Little terns fishing:
hover and plunge
headfirst into water.

Roseate tern: very white,
pink flush below, largely
black bill.

Common tern: dark
tip to bill. Note leg-
length but this and tail-
length not always safe
fieldmarks.

Arctic tern: usually greyer
than common, shorter legs;
tail actually longer than
common.

Little tern: tiny;
yellow legs and bill.

Cormorants: large, all-dark,
white thigh-patches in spring.

From below, **Arctic tern** (far
left) shows light through all
primaries; **common** (left)
has only narrow, semi-
transparent panels.

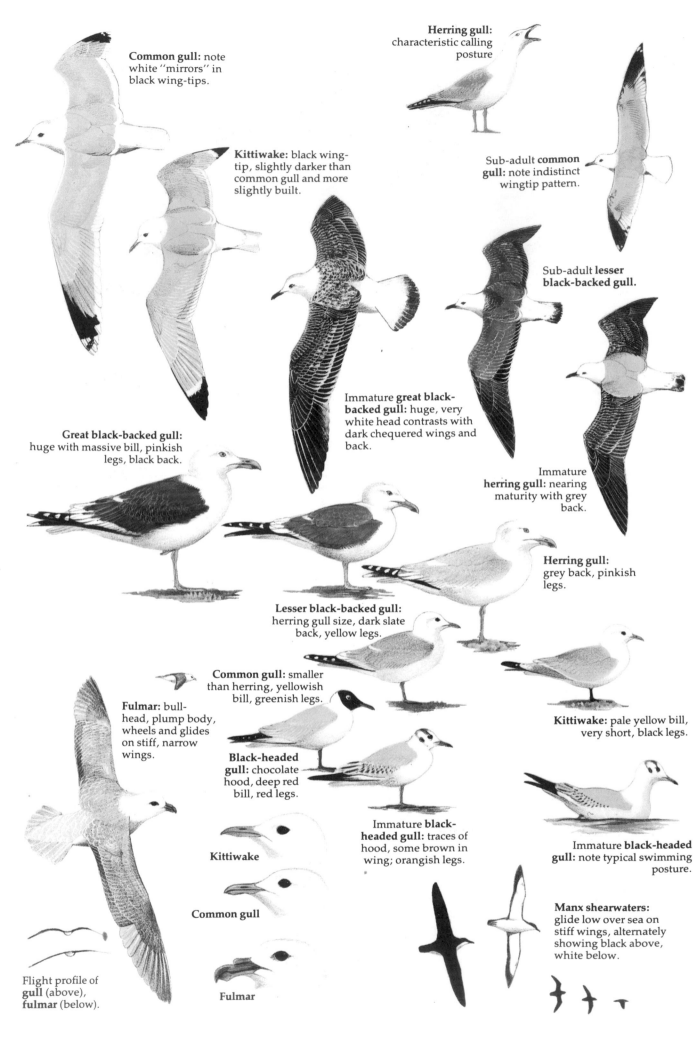

Common gull: note white "mirrors" in black wing-tips.

Herring gull: characteristic calling posture

Kittiwake: black wing-tip, slightly darker than common gull and more slightly built.

Sub-adult **common gull:** note indistinct wingtip pattern.

Sub-adult **lesser black-backed gull.**

Immature **great black-backed gull:** huge, very white head contrasts with dark chequered wings and back.

Great black-backed gull: huge with massive bill, pinkish legs, black back.

Immature **herring gull:** nearing maturity with grey back.

Herring gull: grey back, pinkish legs.

Lesser black-backed gull: herring gull size, dark slate back, yellow legs.

Common gull: smaller than herring, yellowish bill, greenish legs.

Kittiwake: pale yellow bill, very short, black legs.

Fulmar: bull-head, plump body, wheels and glides on stiff, narrow wings.

Black-headed gull: chocolate hood, deep red bill, red legs.

Kittiwake

Immature **black-headed gull:** traces of hood, some brown in wing; orangish legs.

Immature **black-headed gull:** note typical swimming posture.

Common gull

Manx shearwaters: glide low over sea on stiff wings, alternately showing black above, white below.

Flight profile of **gull** (above), **fulmar** (below).

Fulmar

Puffin: greyish cheeks, stands upright on orange legs.

Shape of head and bill best feature for separating **razorbill** (left) and **guillemot** (right) when flying.

Puffin: smaller and longer-winged than other auks, head pattern usually obvious.

Guillemot (left) and **razorbill** (right) leaving cliff: note large, obvious feet.

Razorbill: black and white, distinctive bill shape.

Guillemot: much browner than razorbill; note bill shape.

Distant adult **gannet:** conspicuously white above, black wing-ends.

Adult **gannet:** unmistakable, very large, angular white bird.

Flight profiles of **chough** (top) and **jackdaw** (above).

Ravens: long, rather narrow wings, wedge-shaped tail, massive bill; much larger than crow.

Chough (right): broader wings than **jackdaw** (left), widespread "fingers", no grey on head.

Chough (far left) is blacker than **jackdaw** (left) with red bill and legs.

Shags in summer: dark bottle-green (black at distance), short crest in spring.

Shag (left) slimmer than **cormorant** (right), slighter bill, no white on face.

Rock dove: note white rump panel, dark bars on inner wing; feral pigeon often almost identical. Found extreme north and west of Britain and Ireland.

Eiders: male unmistakable; Female large, dark brown seaduck, angular head and bill, dives.

Black guillemot: all black, small, with white wing-patches, orange legs. Found close inshore.

Razorbill (left): note head-shape, tail often cocked when swimming.
Guillemot (right): looks longer, with larger, finer bill; lower in water.

Puffin: dumpy, greyish cheeks, unique bill.

Gulls

Too often gulls are neglected by birdwatchers. They can, with careful study, be a fascinating group — and if, instead of dismissing a whole flock as the common species, you search through it, there is always the chance of an exciting discovery.

First you must learn the common species in all their different plumages. Using features such as size, leg and bill colours and head and wingtip patterning on birds you see closely, the species can be identified and with this experience you will be able to differentiate between them more and more easily. At a distance shape, flight action, the tone of the upperparts (greatly affected by varying light) and other more subtle features become useful, instead of the specific points, often hard to see, mentioned in the field guides.

Gulls can often be aged with some accuracy through their moult sequences. Spring moult is partial, involving only the feathers on head and body but the autumn moult is complete. This is particularly clear in immature gulls and little gulls, for example, have six distinct plumages before the adult summer plumage is reached.

Little gull:
The world's smallest gull. Pale, with no black on upperside of wings (black beneath may show at rest). Short legs and bill.

Black-headed gull:
Small and pale; dark spot behind eye; red and black bill.

Mediterranean gull:
Like pale, stocky black-headed. Heavy bill. Upswept head patch. White wingtips. Legs and bill black or red.

Adult gulls in winter

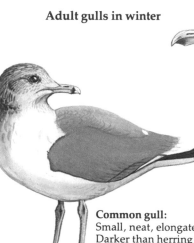

Common gull:
Small, neat, elongated. Darker than herring; green legs. Gentle expression; big dark eye, yellow bill.

Lesser black-backed gull:
Large and dark. Yellow legs, bill and eye.

Glaucous gull:
Large or very large; very pale. White wingtips, pink legs, yellow bill. Iceland has shorter bill, rounder head, more pigeon-like appearance, but plumage similar.

Kittiwake:
Dark head spot and grey nape (lost in summer). Short black legs.

Herring gull:
Large and pale. Heavy yellow bill with red spot. Pink legs.

Great black-backed gull:
Huge. Whiter head than others in winter. Upperparts darker than lesser black-backed. Heavy bill and head. Pink legs and yellow bill.

Herring gull

First year: large, mottled brown with indistinct pattern. Inner primaries often paler than on lesser black-backed gull (below). Browner, less clear-cut than young common gull.

Second year: distinctive pale grey develops on back. Gradual increase of grey in later years, but rate of development variable. May be very pale in summer.

Adult: like large, pale, broad-winged common gull with larger head and red-spotted bill. Pink legs. Pale grey beneath flight feathers. Heavy flight but soars and glides masterfully.

Lesser black-backed gull

First year: like dark herring (above), often more uniform.

Second year: dark grey saddle appears. Pattern and rate of development variable, as in herring.

Adult: darker than herring, greyer than great black-back (below). Dark grey below flight feathers. Yellow legs.

Great black-backed gull

First year: paler than herring, especially on head and body. More boldly chequered. Huge, heavy, broad winged.

Second/third year: variable development of black above.

Adult: black upperparts. Huge, with protruding white head and very heavy bill. Powerful flight.

45

Little gull

The plumage grown before first flight is termed **juvenile** plumage, heavily mottled blackish.

The head and body feathers moult to give a paler **first winter** plumage (*cf* kittiwake, below).

The following spring they moult again to produce **first summer** plumage. Original wing and tail feathers are worn, faded and streaky. Tailband may be broken by new, white feathers.

Spring moult of head and body then gives **second summer** — partial hood.

Whole plumage replaced in late summer to give **second winter** — black spots on grey wingtip.

Complete moult next autumn produces **adult winter** — whole of upperwing pale.

Adult summer — black hood (no white eyelids) and dark bill. Upperwing pale grey, bordered white; underwing blackish. Very small.

Kittiwake

First winter (Compare with little gull) never has dark back and rump of little.

Black nape band obscure by **first summer**. Bird shown here has moulted inner primaries, old outer ones worn and faded, black wing diagonal bleached and partially replaced by grey.

Adult summer: immaculate; primaries paler than mantle and neatly tipped black. Swooping graceful flight.

Black-headed gull

Juvenile: white on outer primaries distinctive; brightly patterned with tawny, black, white and silver-grey.

Adult summer: wings as winter adult, brown hood. Bill and legs darker red.

Adult winter: black and red bill; head spot; white flash on outer primaries. Underside of primaries with white streak. Tail white.

First winter: narrow tailband; head spot, white forewing flash.

Mediterranean gull

First summer: paler, wing pattern less contrasted. White inner webs on primaries showing due to wear. Legs reddish.

First winter: superficially like common in flight (see below) but really more like black-headed. Note head and bill, very pale 'saddle'.

Second winter: head and bill distinctive. Dark spots on tips of pale grey wings.

Adult summer: outstanding bird, with largely whitish wings, brilliant bill and legs, jet black hood with white eyelids.

First summer: becoming very badly worn and faded prior to moult; may gain brownish hood. Very pale overall.

Adult winter: frosty white wingtips. Dark bill and legs (red or black). Upswept head markings.

Common gull

First summer: paler. Wings become less contrasted.

First winter: (see Mediterranean above) neatly marked, rather dark, with dark primaries, grey 'saddle' and clear cut tailband.

Second winter: adult-type grey above with more black, less white on wing. Dark spots on tail rarely obvious.

Adult summer; darker, neater than herring. Smaller head and bill. Greenish legs. Fluent, graceful flight action.

Late first summer: some become very pale prior to moult, largely pale creamy on wings with darker saddle. Considerable individual variation.

Glaucous gull

First winter: variably blotched and barred with brown and cream. Bill large, pale with black tip. Never has black on wingtips or tail, which are cream-coloured.

Iceland gull

First winter (head shown): head more domed, gentler expression. Shorter bill, more pigeon-like appearance. Plumage like glaucous. Bill pattern like glaucous after first year (when darker).

Glaucous gull

Third winter: may have more grey above or paler wings than shown. Rate of development varies individually. Wingtips always very pale.

Shores and estuaries in autumn and winter

Waders, particularly the smaller species, are a very difficult group to learn. Wing- and tail-patterns are the key identification features. Get to know the very common dunlin well and other small waders will be learned more easily. Swimming birds can be identified by their plumage patterns and how they sit in the water. Immature gulls are another difficult group identified by wing- and tail-patterns.

Summer

Winter

Sanderling: small, very white, fast-running. Found on sandy shores.

Little stint: tiny, "tittit" call. Immature (below) has whitish back markings, adult very like small dunlin.

Purple sandpiper: dumpy, short legs, very tame. Found on rocks, breakwaters, etc.

Dunlin: commonest small wader. Note variation — winter adults much paler than immatures. **Sanderling** (bottom) always much whiter in winter.

Curlew sandpiper: similar to dunlin but larger with white rump. Characteristic "chirrip" call.

Turnstone: stocky, dark breast and back, chestnut above in summer. Found on open and rocky shores.

Knot: medium-sized wader, very grey, indistinct wing-bar, greyish rump. See also grey plover.

Dunlin (far left) and immature **little stint:** compare size, back-markings, bills.

Ringed plover: combination of back-colour, wing and tail markings distinguish from other small waders.

Little stints: clean white below, very short bills. Immature (left), winter adult (above).

Turnstone: pied back and wing patterns, twittering call.

Dunlin: variable in plumage, and bill shape and size.

Purple sandpiper: darkest wader, indistinct white markings.

Curlew sandpiper: more slender and slightly larger than dunlin, longer decurved bill.

Knot: larger than other waders on this page, mainly grey in winter, straight bill, rather short legs.

Common sandpiper: note markings, but best told by distinctive flight — flicking on stiffly bowed wings, low over water.

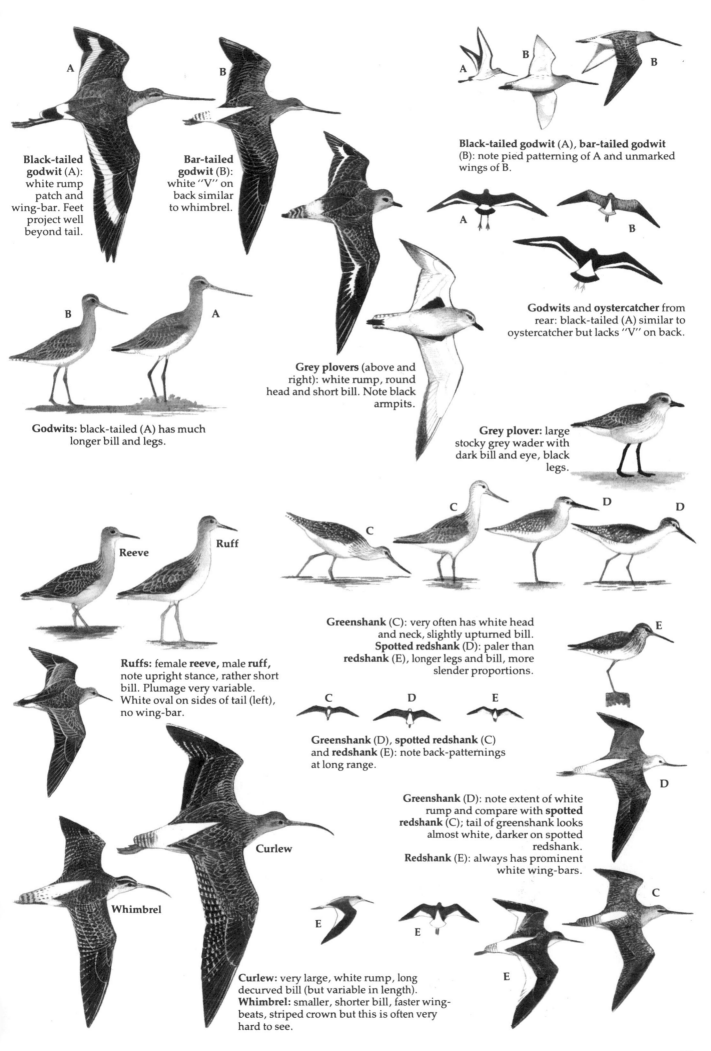

Black-tailed godwit (A): white rump patch and wing-bar. Feet project well beyond tail.

Bar-tailed godwit (B): white "V" on back similar to whimbrel.

Black-tailed godwit (A), bar-tailed godwit (B): note pied patterning of A and unmarked wings of B.

Godwits and **oystercatcher** from rear: black-tailed (A) similar to oystercatcher but lacks "V" on back.

Grey plovers (above and right): white rump, round head and short bill. Note black armpits.

Grey plover: large stocky grey wader with dark bill and eye, black legs.

Godwits: black-tailed (A) has much longer bill and legs.

Ruffs: female **reeve**, male **ruff**, note upright stance, rather short bill. Plumage very variable. White oval on sides of tail (left), no wing-bar.

Greenshank (C): very often has white head and neck, slightly upturned bill.
Spotted redshank (D): paler than **redshank (E)**, longer legs and bill, more slender proportions.

Greenshank (D), spotted redshank (C) and **redshank (E)**: note back-patternings at long range.

Greenshank (D): note extent of white rump and compare with **spotted redshank (C)**; tail of greenshank looks almost white, darker on spotted redshank.
Redshank (E): always has prominent white wing-bars.

Curlew: very large, white rump, long decurved bill (but variable in length).
Whimbrel: smaller, shorter bill, faster wing-beats, striped crown but this is often very hard to see.

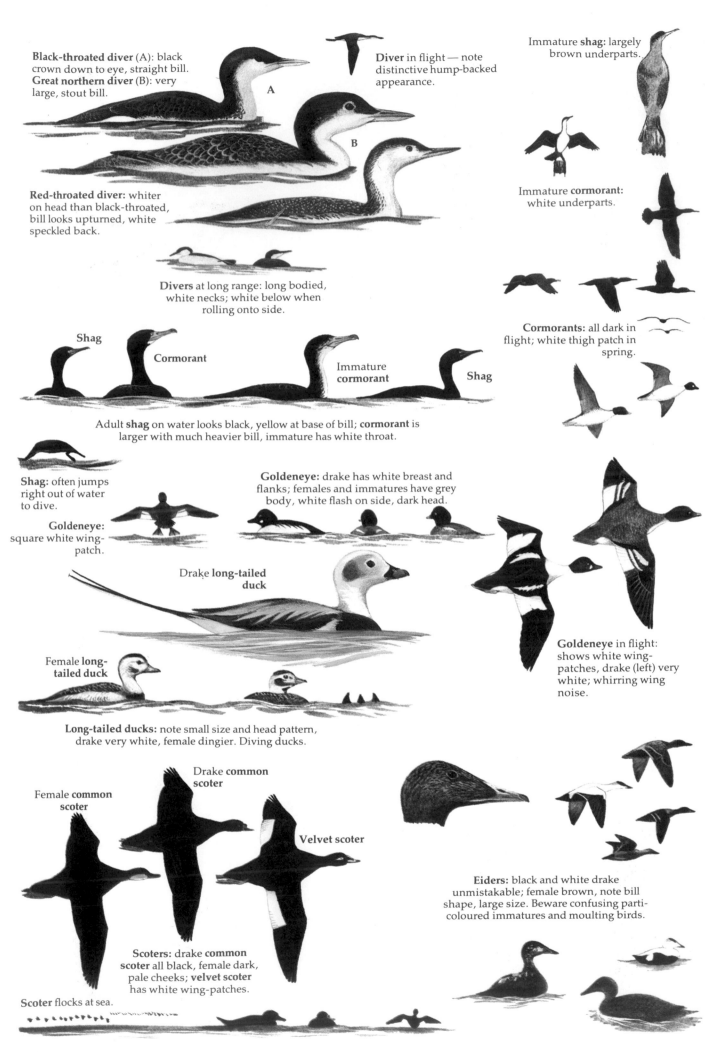

Black-throated diver (A): black crown down to eye, straight bill.
Great northern diver (B): very large, stout bill.

Diver in flight — note distinctive hump-backed appearance.

Immature **shag:** largely brown underparts.

Red-throated diver: whiter on head than black-throated, bill looks upturned, white speckled back.

Immature **cormorant:** white underparts.

Divers at long range: long bodied, white necks; white below when rolling onto side.

Shag
Cormorant
Immature cormorant
Shag

Cormorants: all dark in flight; white thigh patch in spring.

Adult **shag** on water looks black, yellow at base of bill; **cormorant** is larger with much heavier bill, immature has white throat.

Shag: often jumps right out of water to dive.

Goldeneye: square white wing-patch.

Goldeneye: drake has white breast and flanks; females and immatures have grey body, white flash on side, dark head.

Drake **long-tailed duck**

Female **long-tailed duck**

Goldeneye in flight: shows white wing-patches, drake (left) very white; whirring wing noise.

Long-tailed ducks: note small size and head pattern, drake very white, female dingier. Diving ducks.

Drake **common scoter**

Female **common scoter**

Velvet scoter

Eiders: black and white drake unmistakable; female brown, note bill shape, large size. Beware confusing parti-coloured immatures and moulting birds.

Scoters: drake **common scoter** all black, female dark, pale cheeks; **velvet scoter** has white wing-patches.

Scoter flocks at sea.

Oystercatchers flying: unmistakable large, pied waders.

Immature **shelduck:** large whitish, lacks full markings of adult (behind).

Lapwings: pied wader, but note very characteristic wing-shape.

Lapwing: note crest and white sides of head.

Oystercatchers at rest: white chin-mark in winter.

Red-necked grebe: similar to small great crested, but yellowish bill, black crown down to eye, neck often greyish contrasting with white cheeks.

Black-necked and **Slavonian grebes:** postures common to both, dive frequently.

Twite: small, mainly brown, linnet-like finch, yellow bill, some white on wings. Forms flocks.

Brent geese: small bill, black head and neck, dark upper-parts, grey belly. Swimming bird is dark-bellied race.

Slavonian grebe (top), **black-necked** (above): note bill shape and extent of black on crown.

Male **snow bunting**

Brent geese from rear: look all dark, white chevron on tail.

Female **snow bunting**

Skylark

Snow buntings (above and below): males whitest, females dingier, but always have much white on wings. Juvenile (left): much browner, note white on outer tail feathers.

Twite flying up from shore: note unmarked tail, pinkish rump sometimes obvious.

Shore lark

Shore lark: compare pattern of wings and tail with larger browner skylark (above).

Twite (left) and **shore larks** (right and below): note latter's pale underparts and face-markings.

Snow buntings (below): creep low over shore, often feed with twite.

51

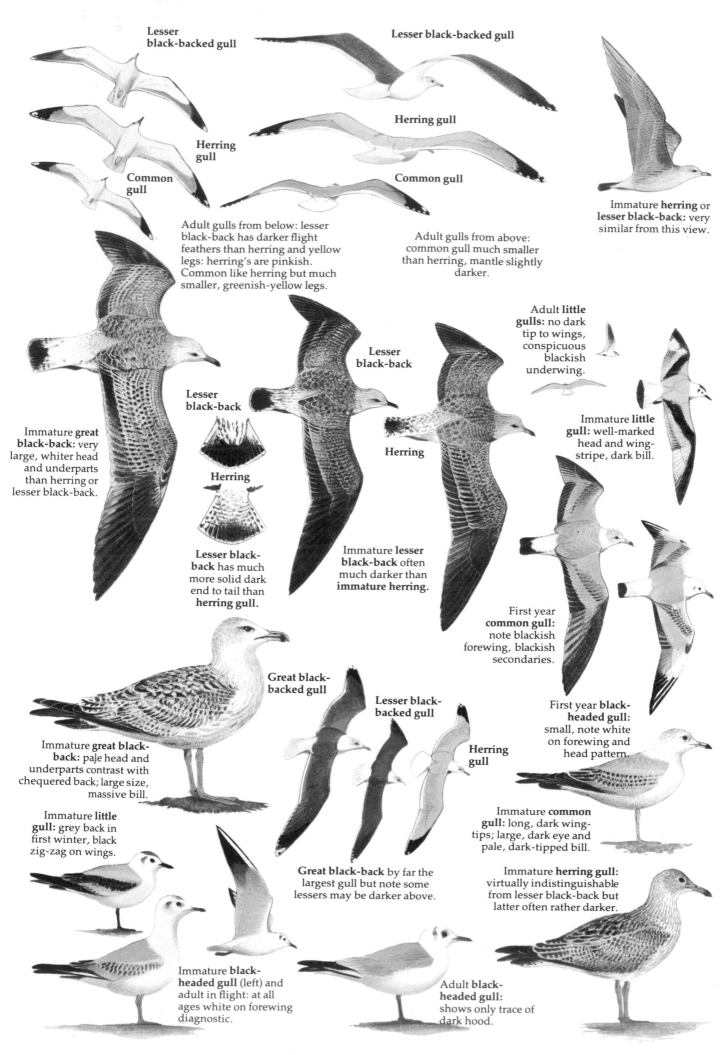

Lesser black-backed gull

Herring gull

Common gull

Lesser black-backed gull

Herring gull

Common gull

Immature **herring** or **lesser black-back**: very similar from this view.

Adult gulls from below: lesser black-back has darker flight feathers than herring and yellow legs; herring's are pinkish. Common like herring but much smaller, greenish-yellow legs.

Adult gulls from above: common gull much smaller than herring, mantle slightly darker.

Adult **little gulls**: no dark tip to wings, conspicuous blackish underwing.

Immature **great black-back**: very large, whiter head and underparts than herring or lesser black-back.

Lesser black-back

Lesser black-back

Herring

Lesser black-back has much more solid dark end to tail than **herring gull**.

Lesser black-back

Herring

Immature **lesser black-back** often much darker than **immature herring**.

Immature **little gull**: well-marked head and wing-stripe, dark bill.

First year **common gull**: note blackish forewing, blackish secondaries.

First year **black-headed gull**: small, note white on forewing and head pattern.

Immature **great black-back**: pale head and underparts contrast with chequered back; large size, massive bill.

Great black-backed gull

Lesser black-backed gull

Herring gull

Great black-back by far the largest gull but note some lessers may be darker above.

Immature **common gull**: long, dark wing-tips; large, dark eye and pale, dark-tipped bill.

Immature **little gull**: grey back in first winter, black zig-zag on wings.

Immature **black-headed gull** (left) and adult in flight: at all ages white on forewing diagnostic.

Adult **black-headed gull**: shows only trace of dark hood.

Immature **herring gull**: virtually indistinguishable from lesser black-back but latter often rather darker.

Inland waters in winter

Colour and shape are the main pointers to birds on the water. Note the way in which species differ in their swimming positions. In flight, look at the patterns of wings and the amount of colour on the undersides.

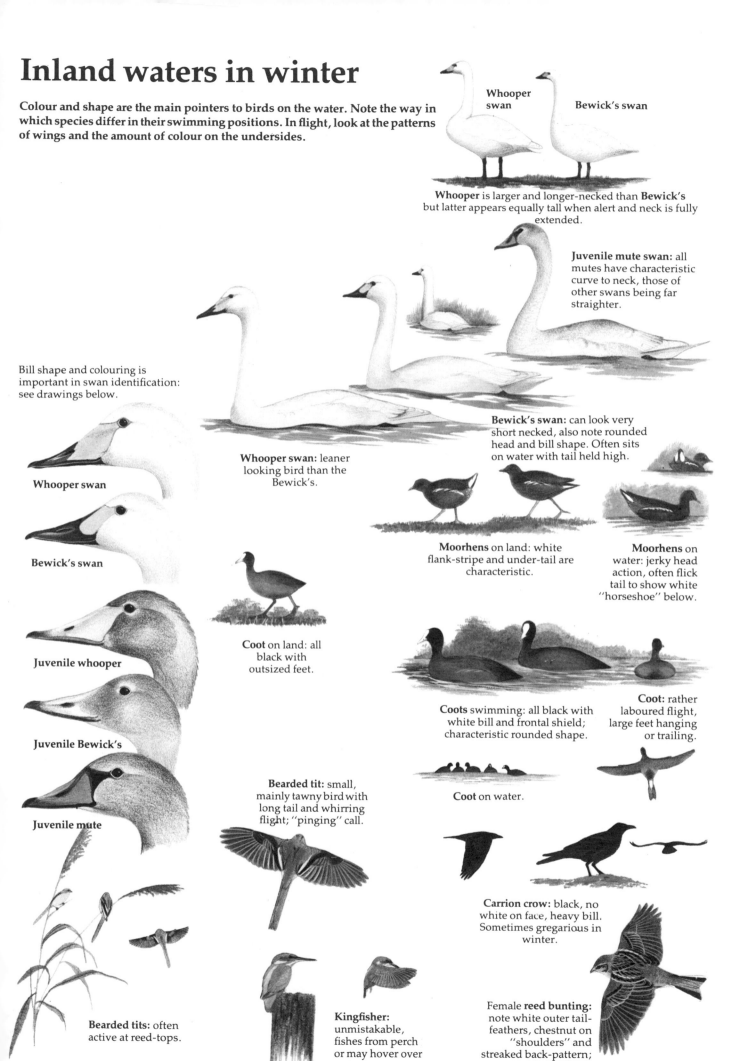

Whooper swan

Bewick's swan

Whooper is larger and longer-necked than **Bewick's** but latter appears equally tall when alert and neck is fully extended.

Juvenile mute swan: all mutes have characteristic curve to neck, those of other swans being far straighter.

Bill shape and colouring is important in swan identification: see drawings below.

Bewick's swan: can look very short necked, also note rounded head and bill shape. Often sits on water with tail held high.

Whooper swan

Bewick's swan

Juvenile whooper

Juvenile Bewick's

Juvenile mute

Whooper swan: leaner looking bird than the Bewick's.

Moorhens on land: white flank-stripe and under-tail are characteristic.

Moorhens on water: jerky head action, often flick tail to show white "horseshoe" below.

Coot on land: all black with outsized feet.

Coots swimming: all black with white bill and frontal shield; characteristic rounded shape.

Coot: rather laboured flight, large feet hanging or trailing.

Coot on water.

Bearded tit: small, mainly tawny bird with long tail and whirring flight; "pinging" call.

Carrion crow: black, no white on face, heavy bill. Sometimes gregarious in winter.

Bearded tits: often active at reed-tops.

Kingfisher: unmistakable, fishes from perch or may hover over water.

Female **reed bunting:** note white outer tail-feathers, chestnut on "shoulders" and streaked back-pattern; jerky flight.

Drake **smew:** unmistakable black-and-white pattern.

Red-breasted merganser (top) and **goosander:** much larger, longer-bodied than smew.

"Redhead": female or juvenile smew; small and compact, white cheeks and breast, small, dark bill.

Drake **smew:** very white.

Female or immature **smew:** red-brown crown, white cheeks and breast, greyish body.

Redhead **smew:** note white on wing-coverts and throat.

Drake **smew**

Female or immature **goldeneye:** white patch on hindwing, all dark head.

Drake **pochard:** wings all grey, black tail and neck, russet head.

Drake **wigeon:** conspicuous white flash on forewing.

Pintails: note characteristic tail-shape and very slender necks.

Pintails

Duck **wigeon:** looks uniformly dark above.

Drake **pintail** from below: distinctive shape and white belly, breast and neck.

Drake **tufted duck:** black-and-white, with broad white wing-bar.

Duck

Drake

Wigeon: both male and female show distinctive white underparts.

Drake

Drake

Duck

Wigeon

Duck

Drake **wigeon:** note white belly, rather short neck and small bill.

Wigeon on water: rather compact with small bills; female rufous but shows white on flanks and below tail.

Wigeon: spend much time ashore, white underparts clearly visible.

Duck **pintail:** slender, long-necked with pointed tail.

Drake **pintail:** white breast and neck visible at very long range.

Pink-footed goose: note grey forewing, very dark head and small bill.

Greylag goose: greyish-white forewing, head and neck uniformly coloured.

Duck **gadwall:** note white wing-patch and whitish belly when seen from below.

Adult **whitefront:** black barring on belly.

White-fronted goose: uniformly coloured, "brownest" grey goose; white on forehead often conspicuous.

Duck **teal:** very small, looks all-dark with white wing-bar.

Duck **shoveler:** pale, blue-grey forewing; large, heavy bill.

Cormorants: large, all dark (but immature has whitish throat), heavy, tilted-up bills.

Red-throated diver: white throat and neck in winter; characteristic "up-tilted" shape to bill.

Shags: more slender necked and finer billed than cormorant. Often jump clear of water before diving, unlike divers.

Great crested grebes: note low and high profile.

Great crested grebe: pink bill, black crown does not extend down to eye.

Herons in flight: large broad wings and deep, slow wing-beats; neck retracted, feet trail beyond tail.

Herons: perched head hunched into shoulders, upright stance.

Great crested grebe in flight: characteristic wing-pattern and trailing feet.

Black-necked grebe

Slavonian grebe

Slavonian grebe shows less white on wing than **black-necked,** and sometimes small white "shoulder patches".

Little grebe: tiny, dumpy build, pale on neck and flanks.

Slavonian grebe: small size, very white cheeks and neck.

Black-necked grebe: less well-defined cap, dingier cheeks and sides of neck.

Dipper: white bib, stocky build, white eyelid often conspicuous.

Dippers: open wings while feeding on water; rapid, low flight on small dark, short wings.

Meadow pipit: white outer-tail feathers in flight; often circles up calling "tseep-tseep" when flushed.

Meadow pipit: streaked brown back, white outer tail feathers.

Snipe: "towers" when flushed, zig-zags up and away; harsh calls.

Jack snipe: flushes at close range, soon drops down again; silent.

Jack snipe: smaller, darker, shorter billed than snipe, with well-patterned back; lacks white on edge of wing and tail.

Jack snipe

Snipe

Water rail when flushed: looks all dark, weak flight, trailing legs.

Juvenile **pied wagtail:** shows only traces of adult's head pattern.

Snipe from below: Jack snipe has plain underwing, much shorter bill, shorter legs.

Water rail "end-on": remarkably slender, note buffish-white undertail.

Water rail: in poor view long bill and rather dark appearance diagnostic; barring on flank often visible.

Jack snipe on ground: very small and dumpy, with peculiar bouncing feeding action.

Ducks in eclipse

GO TO a stretch of water in mid-summer and the chances are that all the ducks you see are females — or are they?

Dabbling ducks
Drakes, in contrast with their dowdy mates, are usually colourful creatures, but this is not always so. In high summer many dabbling ducks are brown and look, at a casual glance, to be female. Towards the end of the breeding season ducks moult, and shed their primary feathers all at once, becoming flightless for a short period. The drakes are said to "go into eclipse", assuming a dull plumage which gives them the protection of camouflage at a time when they are particularly vulnerable to predators. The brilliant feathers are resumed in another moult later in the year. Size, shape, neck length and bill shape all become important when identifying the actual species but separating the drake from the duck can be more of a problem. Although the eclipse plumage of the drake is very like that of the duck, the two are not identical, for the often markedly different wing patterns of the sexes remain. So a brown duck in summer, stretching, preening or otherwise showing a wing, should present no great problem of identification. In addition, there are other (admittedly often subtle) differences, so that given a good view of the bird, it is rarely necessary to see a wing in order to determine whether it be eclipse drake or duck.

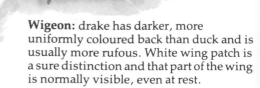

Wigeon: drake has darker, more uniformly coloured back than duck and is usually more rufous. White wing patch is a sure distinction and that part of the wing is normally visible, even at rest.

Shoveler: like wigeon, shoveler drake has darker, more uniform back than duck and is more rufous on underparts. Bright blue wing patch not always visible at rest, but is a sure indication of the drake.

Mallard: note drake's dull, greenish bill, darker back, breast with crimson-purple gloss.

Teal: separation of sexes is difficult; view of wing necessary. Drake has grey-brown forewing and broad, buff-coloured bar before green and black speculum. Duck's forewing is brown, mottled, and band before speculum is narrower and white.

Garganey: virtually impossible to differentiate between sexes in the field unless wing is seen. Lavender-grey patch on drake's forewing and bright green speculum are clearly different from duck's duller wing. Compare with teal above.

Gadwall: most certain distinction is the wing. Drake has clearly defined areas of chestnut, black and white; female has smaller white patch, dark grey in place of black, little or no chestnut.

Pintail: drake is greyer, more evenly coloured bird than duck, lacking boldly patterned upperparts and warm buff shade of head. His bill is blue and black; the duck's is slate-grey.

Diving ducks
When considering diving ducks it must be remembered that ducks as well as drakes have an "eclipse" plumage. It is only marginally different from the breeding plumage and it is often assumed later than the drake's and sometimes for a shorter period. The ducks are shown here in breeding plumage, but some of the minor distinctions apparent in the illustrations are obscured when the duck is also in eclipse; for example, the white collar of the female goldeneye disappears. Only those distinguishing features applicable to all adult female plumages are mentioned in the captions.

Tufted duck: bold black and white pattern of the tufted drake is obscured and much of his crest is lost, but he remains a blackish bird whereas the female is always brown.

Pochard: in the distance drake looks like female, but has uniform, more chestnut head. Note red eye and parti-coloured bill.

Goldeneye: drake retains much larger white wing patch, duck's being smaller and broken. If wing not visible, drake can usually be recognised by darker, less chestnut and differently shaped head, darker back and absence of yellow on bill.

N.W.CUSA.

Smew: very unlikely to be seen in Britain in eclipse plumage. Except in a close view on the water, distinction is hardly possible. Well seen, the drake in eclipse has a chestnut crown, no black about the eye and a darker back.

Scaup: very unlikely to be seen in Britain in high summer. Drake remains blackish in contrast to brown female. Whitish patches about the bill and cheeks, are never so large and clearcut as those of female.

Eider: drake becomes nearly all black save for broad, white patch on wing which at once distinguishes him in flight. Duck is at all seasons a brown bird.

Goosander: drake told from duck at all seasons in flight by greater amount of white in wing. This may or may not be apparent on the water. In eclipse he has a paler head, smaller crest, darker back and paler flanks.

Red-breasted merganser: drake has more white in wing than duck. On the water distinction is not easy — drake has darker, blackish back, smaller crest and lacks white line from bill to eye nearly always apparent in female. Note drake's red eyes.

N.W.CUSA.

Inland waters in spring and summer

Lakes, gravel-pits, rivers, streams and marshes are all good places to see birds. Waterside vegetation in summer is the breeding place of several small perching birds, which can be sorted out by voice and behaviour as well as appearance.

Sedge warbler: typically sings from perch, often hidden in vegetation. But in song-flight (above left) rises and "parachutes" down.

Sedge warbler: creamy stripe over eye, streaked back and tawny rump. Breeds in vegetation bordering water.

Reed warblers: uniformly coloured above, paler below. Breed in reeds, osiers and waterside vegetation.

Grasshopper warbler: note rounded tail and streaked back.

Grasshopper warbler: more often heard than seen, long reeling song on one note.

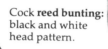

Cock **reed bunting:** black and white head pattern.

Bearded tits: small, very long-tailed tawny birds of reedbeds, male (far right) with grey head and strikingly patterned back; "pinging" calls.

Hen **reed bunting:** pattern of cheeks and moustachial stripe.

Reed bunting: in flight rather jerky, note obvious outer tail-feathers.

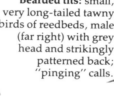

Grey wagtail: slender, very long tail, vivid yellow under-parts. Male has black throat in summer. Found near fast-moving streams.

Yellow wagtails: note white outer tail feathers also visible in flight (below left).

Grey wagtails: undulating flight, note yellow rump and under tail.

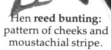

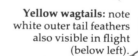

Little ringed plover (far left): smaller than **ringed plover** (left), more white on forehead and narrower breast band.

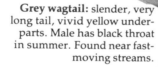

Yellow wagtail: olive above, more uniformly yellow below than grey wagtail and much shorter tail. Single "tseep" call. Found in wet meadows and around gravel pits.

Ringed plover: more black on forehead, yellow on bill and orange-yellow legs. Occasionally breeds on gravel pits but more a coastal bird.

Little ringed plover: white border to crown, yellow eye-ring, almost all-dark bill and legs flesh or greenish-yellow. Often breeds inland on shingle edges of gravel pits and reservoirs.

Little ringed plover: (left): lacks wing bar.

Herony: **herons** are colonial breeders, building large nests in treetops.

Heron: large, long-legged and long-necked with dagger-shaped bill. Although usually seen beside water, does perch in trees.

Herons: in flight; note large round-ended wings, retracted neck, feet projected beyond tail; slow, heavy wing-beats.

Greylag goose: note heavy bill and uniform colour of head, neck and underparts. Birds seen in summer in England are feral.

Canada goose: grey-brown with black neck and head and distinctive markings. Found on lakes, gravel pits and broad rivers, grazes on farmland.

Canada goose: (rear view) landing, note tail pattern and uniformly dark wings.

Greylag: in flight, note off-white forewings.

Snipe: gives short rasping call when flushed and rapidly zigzags away, often climbing high. Found marshes and wet meadows.

Dipper: rear view, fast direct flight, dumpy on short wings.

Dipper: feeds in or under swift-flowing water, even where it is quite deep.

Snipe: "drumming" display-flight has climax in near-vertical dives with a rapid beating produced by vibrating outer tail-feathers.

Kingfisher: note brilliant colours, short tail, large head and bill. May hover like big hummingbird before diving, but more often fishes from perch above water.

Mute swan with cygnets: latter are ash-grey or, very rarely, white.

Sand martin: note contrast between upper side and under side.

Mute swan: note raised wings, curved neck and knob at base of orange (or pinkish) bill. Basal knob on female is smaller.

Great crested grebe: striped young often ride on parent's back.

Little grebe or **dabchick:** tiny, round-bodied, looks all-dark at distance or in poor light. Dives when disturbed. Found lakes, rivers and gravel pits.

Great crested grebe: dives from surface for fish. Note head-plumage and slender white neck. Found broad rivers, lakes and gravel pits.

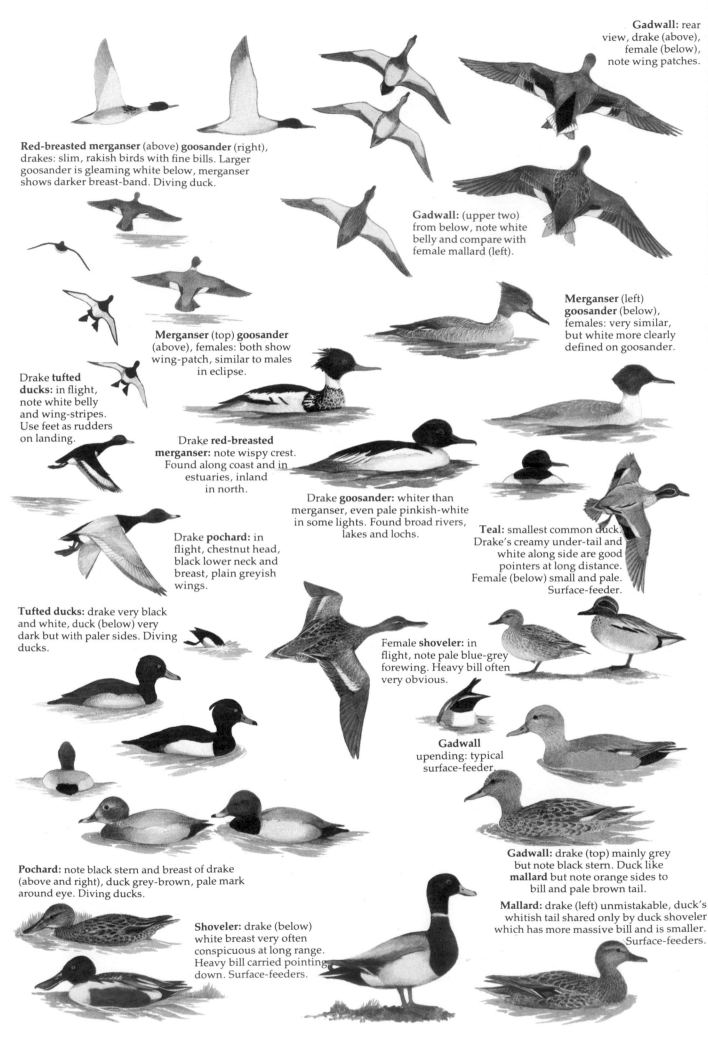

Gadwall: rear view, drake (above), female (below), note wing patches.

Red-breasted merganser (above) **goosander** (right), drakes: slim, rakish birds with fine bills. Larger goosander is gleaming white below, merganser shows darker breast-band. Diving duck.

Gadwall: (upper two) from below, note white belly and compare with female mallard (left).

Merganser (left) **goosander** (below), females: very similar, but white more clearly defined on goosander.

Merganser (top) **goosander** (above), females: both show wing-patch, similar to males in eclipse.

Drake **tufted ducks:** in flight, note white belly and wing-stripes. Use feet as rudders on landing.

Drake **red-breasted merganser:** note wispy crest. Found along coast and in estuaries, inland in north.

Drake **goosander:** whiter than merganser, even pale pinkish-white in some lights. Found broad rivers, lakes and lochs.

Teal: smallest common duck. Drake's creamy under-tail and white along side are good pointers at long distance. Female (below) small and pale. Surface-feeder.

Drake **pochard:** in flight, chestnut head, black lower neck and breast, plain greyish wings.

Tufted ducks: drake very black and white, duck (below) very dark but with paler sides. Diving ducks.

Female **shoveler:** in flight, note pale blue-grey forewing. Heavy bill often very obvious.

Gadwall upending: typical surface-feeder.

Pochard: note black stern and breast of drake (above and right), duck grey-brown, pale mark around eye. Diving ducks.

Gadwall: drake (top) mainly grey but note black stern. Duck like **mallard** but note orange sides to bill and pale brown tail.

Mallard: drake (left) unmistakable, duck's whitish tail shared only by duck shoveler which has more massive bill and is smaller. Surface-feeders.

Shoveler: drake (below) white breast very often conspicuous at long range. Heavy bill carried pointing down. Surface-feeders.

Continental birds — freshwater and coastal habitats

Many of the birds associated with freshwater and coastal habitats are very distinctive and should present few problems. Take care, however, with the gulls and warblers.

White stork — often soars

Grey heron (left) and **purple heron** (right) — note colour and deep keel of **purple heron**

White stork flies with neck outstretched

From below, **night heron** is pale, dumpy with rounded wings

Purple heron — note dark appearance, neck pattern

White storks: marshes, wet meadows; nest on buildings and trees

Night heron (left and below): small, dumpy, note black crown and back

Purple heron looks darker and more angular than **grey heron**

Female **little bittern** going away

Male **little bittern:** tiny, unique pattern

Flamingos — very tall, slender, long neck and legs

Female little bittern: rising from cover

Squacco heron — small, short-necked; buff back, white wings

Flamingos flying; note dingy juvenile

Slender-billed gull (left): white head, longish neck and bill — compare **black-headed** (right)

Eye of **slender-billed gull** can look dark. Note bill

Black-headed gull

Audouin's gull

Slender-billed and **black-headed gulls** approaching

Note long-headed appearance of **slender-billed gull**

Black-winged stilt flying (above and below): unmistakable

Black-winged stilts male (left) female (right). Note length of legs!

Audouin's gull: note long head, red bill, dark eye

Gull-billed terns: large, short tail, short black bill

Mediterranean herring gull — yellow legs

Red-crested pochards — unmistakable. Note duck's pale cheeks

Ferruginous ducks (drake right) — note colour, white sterns

Audouin's gull shows less white at wingtips, shorter tail than **herring,** and narrower white rear edge to wing

Male **marsh harrier:** dark body, grey flight feathers tipped black, grey tail

Female **marsh harrier;** very dark, creamy head and forewing

Approaching female **marsh harrier:** note head, legs, angle of wings

Female **marsh harrier** low over reeds

Approaching **osprey:** note kinked, gull-like wings

Osprey dives obliquely, enters water feet-first. "Shakes" on rising

Osprey above — distinct pattern (note head), very long wings

Male **marsh harrier** — unique colour combination

Eleonora's falcon — dark above, long-winged

Eleonora's falcon is large, rakish, agile falcon Light form

Dark form **Eleonora's falcon** — uniform sooty-black. Both forms occur together

Eleonora's falcon — note underwing and body colours, dark upper surfaces

Smaller **hobby** is paler

Eleonora's falcon breeds colonially on cliffs *eg* Mallorca. Nests late summer

Eleonora's falcon is sociable: often feeds on wing

Great reed warbler (right & below) — starling size, conspicuous, loud harsh song

Reed warbler — mainly reedbeds, but also other damp habitats

Marsh warbler — mainly semi-wet and even dry places; less warm, more uniform colour than **reed**, paler face — but separation difficult

Reed warbler — shown in upright pose (also used by **marsh**)

Cetti's warbler: very skulking: short explosive song. Earth-brown, rounded tail

Great reed — crashing heavily into cover

Sedge warbler — passage only in this region

Savi's warbler: reeling song. Compare head and tail with reed (above)

Fan-tailed warbler: tiny, short-tailed. Note tail markings

Moustached warbler (lower two) — darker crown, whiter supercilium, rather darker overall, shorter wing. Note darker flank colour

Fan-tailed warbler has dancing song flight 'zeep-zeep-zeep' monotonously

Continental birds — inland habitats

Most birds of prey will be seen 'inland' — trips into the hinterland away from the beach, especially where there are hills or mountains, will be very rewarding. The very rare black vulture is probably more easily seen in Mallorca than anywhere else in Europe. Keep a sharp eye open for continental species of larks, and wagtails that differ slightly from their British counterparts.

Griffon (G) and **black vultures** (B) are vast soaring birds: **black** is all dark, normally soaring on flat wings like airborne plank; **griffon** shows much more contrast and is likely to be seen in numbers in suitable areas.

Griffon vultures (above and below right): note huge size, contrasting dark flight feathers.

Red kite: note tail.

Adult **Egyptian vultures:** dirty white, black flight features, small head, fine bill.

Immature **Egyptian:** much smaller than **black:** note tail shape, fine bill.

Red kite: long wings, forked chestnut tail, pale head.

Immature **Egyptian vulture.**

Adult **Egyptian vulture.**

Black kites: sombre plumage, paler wing coverts, tail much less forked.

Red kites: note whitish wing-panel; tail flexes and twists.

Compare shape of **lesser kestrel** (left) with female **kestrel** (right).

From below, male **lesser kestrel** has very pale underwing; smallish head, narrow tail.

Male **lesser kestrel:** bright colours, grey-blue band across upper wing.

Female **lesser kestrel:** rather small head, often greyer rump than **kestrel** darker wingtips.

Little egret: small, slender, black bill and legs, yellow feet

Cattle egret: dumpy, rounded wings: dark legs late summer/autumn

Cattle egret: summer: buff on crown and back; note pale bill and legs, heavy jowl

Little egret: slimmer, all white; note bill and yellow feet

Cory's shearwater: big, brownish above, whitish below; rather slow but typical shearwater flight action — gliding on stiffly-held wings

Male **Kentish plover:** small, slim, very pale, sparingly marked; black legs

Ringed plover for comparison

Female **Kentish plover:** even more sparingly marked than male

Mediterranean **herring gull:** note yellow rather than pink legs

Roller: beautiful pattern of light and dark blues in flight; chestnut back

Bee-eaters: very aerial, hawking insects; constant "prruip" calls

Note distinctive shapes of wings and tail

Roller: unmistakable; uses prominent perch in open

Hoopoe: floppy action, broad rounded wings

Hoopoe: unmistakable combination of cinnamon, black and white

Hoopoe: flops away with characteristic action.

At rest, **bee-eaters** are unmistakable

Note coppery underwing

Great grey shrike: largest shrike. Southern birds darker than in north, pinkish on breast

Woodchat shrike flying away — unmistakable pattern

Woodchat shrike: unmistakable — but much dingier by late summer

Great grey: note amounts of black and white

Lesser grey shrike: smaller, paler; usually black across forehead; note rather short, deep bill

Lesser grey: paler, different wing pattern

Male red-backed shrike: grey head, chestnut back

Great grey shrike

Lesser grey shrike

Woodchats from front and rear

Male red-backed: note grey rump, tail pattern

Female red-backed shrike: variable; lacks male's bright plumage; often browner than this

Male black redstart: rooftops, rocky areas etc. Note reddish tail

Female black redstart: much dingier and often paler than this

Female red-backed: looks plain brown with long tail

Serins flushed: note yellow rumps

Scops owl: very small owl with direct, not undulating flight

Serins: often on wires. Constant metallic twittering and singing

Male serin: small, streaky, yellow head and rump

Scops owl: very small, slim, "eared". Repetitive "pew . . . pew . . ." song

69

Skylark: white rear edge to wing, white outer tail feathers

Short-toed lark: white outer tail feathers; sparrowlike flight call

Crested lark: loping flight, short tail buff at sides, broad wings

Indistinctly marked **short-toed lark:** not unlike sparrow. Walks — not hops

Short-toed lark: painted to same scale as Thekla and crested larks below

Thekla lark: often greyer than crested, more heavily marked on breast, shorter bill, shorter crest

Crested lark: note longish bill, long crest; breast usually finely streaked

Short-toed lark: small size, reddish crown, often suggestion of dark mark at sides of neck

Male **blue-headed wagtail:** looks dark from rear; "tsweeep" call

Male **blue-headed wagtail:** note grey-blue head, supercilium

'Yellow' wagtails: shorter tails than other wagtails

Thekla lark: greyish underwing

Crested lark: orange-buff underwing

Female **Spanish wagtail:** shorter supercilium than blue-headed

Female **Sardinian warbler:** small, dark, white throat, long tail

White wagtail: much paler and greyer than pied — note grey rump

Male **Sardinian:** dark with black head and long tail

White **wagtail:** less black than on **pied**

Firecrest: bright green and whitish — note head pattern

Male **Sardinian warbler:** long tail, black head, red eye, white throat

Female **Sardinian:** looks all-dark, long tail, white throat

Goldcrest for comparison; usually hill woods only

Over the next four pages you will find some more Mediterranean specialities. Study the larks, buntings and warblers carefully — compare them with earlier pages. In many cases familiar British species will also be present. Don't overlook the sparrows and starlings, which are not *all* the same as those at home.

Juvenile **great spotted cuckoo:** black cap, white on wings. **Magpie** is usual foster parent

Juvenile **great spotted cuckoo:** chestnut primaries, white on outer tail

Adult for comparison.

Adult **great spotted cuckoo:** white on back, wings and tail

Quail — tiny, sandy gamebird, seldom seen

Female **black-eared wheatear** — note body colour, unmarked face

Male **black-eared wheatear** — very pale, black face and wings

Black-eared wheatears: autumn female above left, autumn male below left, spring male right

Flying **quail** is small, long-winged; almost snipe-like flight

Calandra larks (left and above): big, bulky, long wings dark below. Black spots at sides of breast

Woodlarks (right and above) — superb song from exposed perch or on wing, creamy eyestripe, broad wings, very short tail

71

Red-rumped swallow: note collar, rump, tail shape

Compare shape and colours with **swallow** (right). **Red-rumped swallow** lacks throat and white tail markings

Swallow and three **red-rumped swallows** overhead

Red-rumped swallow has distinctive long-tailed shape

At rest, seen well, **red-rumped swallow** is unmistakable

Short-toed treecreeper has dusky flanks — but best told by tit-like calls; not found at higher altitudes

Crested tit — distinctive crest and face pattern. Not confined to conifers

Crested tit above: note bib pattern

Short-toed treecreeper — like treecreeper, shows wing bar in flight

Seen well, **wryneck** is unmistakable. Almost reptilian appearance

Flying **wryneck** has pointed head, shortish tail, dipping flight

Spotless starling — Spain, Portugal, Corsica, Sardinia: dark, glossy, no spots

Spotless starling — usually singly or in small groups

Wryneck flying away — note back pattern. Tail may also be browner. Below — often feeds on ground

Hawfinch — dumpy, big-headed, huge bill. Note head colour, grey nape, white on wings (especially in flight), white tip to short tail

Hawfinch — showing white on wings and tail; and unique shape of secondary feathers

Distant male **ortolan** — note "moustaches" and underparts colour, greyish head

Ortolan in flight — longish tail, narrow wings. Female (left) shows pale eye-ring and bill

Female **cirl bunting** — broader winged, shorter-tailed than **ortolan**

Ortolan — note colours of head, breast and belly

Male **cirl bunting** — distinctive head pattern

Female **cirl bunting** — rather nondescript — no pale eye ring

Female **ortolan** going away — looks fairly uniform

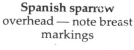

Spanish sparrow overhead — note breast markings

Spanish sparrows (left and below) — very heavily marked black below, down to sides of breast

Italian race of **house sparrow** (right) has brown cap

Bonelli's warbler from below— whitish underparts

Bonelli's warbler — yellowish rump

Bonelli's warbler — looks pale-headed, whitish below

Melodious warblers (left) — green and yellow, shortish wings. Woods, scrub, gardens etc. Varied, rather unmelodious song!

Bonelli's is whitish below — wood warbler has similar trilling song but very yellow on breast

Orphean warbler from below — white throat, black cap, pale eye

Spectacled warbler — male: like small, bright, dark-cheeked whitethroat; low scrub, especially *Salicornia* at coast

Orphean warblers (above and right) — big, black-headed, pale eye. Woodland. Thrush-like song

Female **spectacled warbler** — duller. Both sexes have very pale legs

Rufous bush chat — bold, conspicuous; droops wings, erects and fans tail

Juvenile **spectacled warbler** — browner, whitish below. No grey on head

Rufous bush chat — distinctive chestnut tail tipped black and white

Rufous bush chat — slim and long-legged

Continental birds — upland habitats

Most typical upland birds are, fortunately, well marked and readily identified. Also included here are some of the trickier birds of prey. As always with raptors, shape and relative proportions are as important as plumage colours and patterns.

Choughs — broad wings, acrobatic flight

Chough — decurved red bill
Note shapes of flying **choughs** — both are similar: note bill shapes and colours. Different voices — **Chough:** "kyow", and **Alpine chough** "chirrish" calls

Chough (above), **Alpine chough** (below) — both have red legs, but note **Alpine's** yellow bill. **Alpine** usually at higher elevations

Alpine swift — large size, white below, dark throat band

Jackdaw for comparison. Compare wing and bill shape

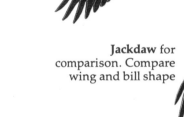

Black woodpeckers (l and rt) — hill woods, especially beech and pine, crow size. Male has more red on crown. Note distinctive head shape

Pallid swift — paler, more white at throat, slightly broader wings

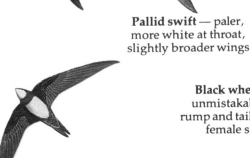

Alpine swift

Black wheatear — unmistakable; note rump and tail. Male and female similar

Male **rock thrush** is unmistakable

Female **rock thrush** — browner, but note red tail

Crag martins — note shape, dingy colour, tail markings

Male **rock thrush** — white on back very variable in extent

Compare **crag** (left) with **sand martin** (rt)

Female **rock thrush** — note short red tail

Blue rock thrush — male uniform slate-blue

Male **blue rock thrush** (above): female (left) much duller

Rock sparrows — note head and tail markings, yellow breast spot

Juvenile **rock bunting** — note face pattern, rump

Barbary partridge

Red-legged partridge

Rock partridge

Barbary partridge Gibraltar and Sardinia only, compare carefully face and flank patterns of **rock** and **red-legged**

Rock bunting — chestnut below, distinctive head markings

Distant **goshawk**

Adult **goshawk** — very large, short broad wings, white under tail

Immature **honey buzzard** — note wing and tail patterns

Immature **goshawk** — note streaks on breast, tail pattern

Hobby — rakish shape, characteristic face and underparts pattern

Goshawk going away

All-dark **honey buzzards**

Very pale **honey buzzard**

Honey buzzards: soar and glide on flat wings

Well marked **honey buzzard** and distant migrants. Note long tail, tail pattern, cuckoo-like head

Male **Montagu's harrier** (above) — distinctive underwing pattern. Juvenile (below) strikingly chestnut underparts

Female **Montagu's** (above) — note face markings — often pale coverts. Male (below) — note black bar on wing, tail pattern

Short-toed eagle from behind and high above: often hovers

Typical **short-toed**: very large, very white, dark breast and large, owlish head

Short-toed eagle going away

Short-toed eagle — looks all dark above

Adult **Bonelli's** — very white body, dark wings — note tail pattern

Adult **Bonelli's eagle** — dark, variable white on back; note tail. Profile below

Immature **Bonelli's** — note sandy undersides, pale flight feathers. Note "eagle shape" in small drawing

Pale **booted eagle** — smaller than **Bonelli's**, whiter, white under wings

Dark booted eagles — longer tail, more uniform than **buzzard**. May "stoop" from height

Dark booted eagle (below)

Immature **booted eagle** (right) differs from **Bonelli's** in dark flight feathers

Immature **booted** — often shows paler coverts, some white on rump

Index